Sources for the study of crim   , 1001–1921

Maynooth Research Guides for Irish Local History

GENERAL EDITOR Mary Ann Lyons

This book is one of the Maynooth Research Guides for Irish Local History series. Written by specialists in the relevant fields, these volumes are designed to provide historians, and specifically those interested in local history, with practical advice regarding the consultation of specific collections of historical material, thereby enabling them to conduct independent research in a competent and thorough manner. In each volume, a brief history of the relevant institutions is provided and the principal primary sources are identified and critically evaluated, with specific reference to their usefulness to the local historian. Readers receive step by step guidance as to how to conduct their research and are alerted to some of the problems which they might encounter in working with particular collections. Possible avenues for research are suggested and relevant secondary works are also recommended.

The General Editor acknowledges the assistance of both Dr Raymond Gillespie, NUI Maynooth and Dr James Kelly, St Patrick's College, Drumcondra, in the preparation of this book for publication.

IN THIS SERIES

Terence A.M. Dooley, *Sources for the history of landed estates in Ireland* (Irish Academic Press, 2000)

Raymond Refaussé, *Church of Ireland records* (Irish Academic Press, 2000)

Patrick J. Corish and David C. Sheehy, *Records of the Irish Catholic Church* (Irish Academic Press, 2001)

Philomena Connolly, *Medieval record sources* (Four Courts Press, 2002)

Brian Gurrin, *Pre-census sources for Irish demography* (Four Courts Press, 2002)

E. Margaret Crawford, *Counting the people: a survey of the Irish censuses, 1813–1911* (Four Courts Press, 2003)

Brian Hanley, *A guide to Irish military heritage, 1813–1911* (Four Courts Press, 2004).

Jacinta Prunty, *Maps and map-making in local history* (Four Courts Press, 2004)

Brian Griffin, *Sources for the study of crime in Ireland, 1801–1921* (Four Courts Press, 2005)

Toby Barnard, *A guide to the sources for Irish material culture, 1500–2000* (Four Courts Press, forthcoming)

Maynooth Research Guides for Irish Local History: Number 9

Sources for the study of crime in Ireland, 1801–1921

Brian Griffin

FOUR COURTS PRESS

Set in 10.5 pt on 12.5 pt Bembo for
FOUR COURTS PRESS LTD
7 Malpas Street, Dublin 8, Ireland
e-mail: info@four-courts-press.ie
http://www.four-courts-press.ie
and in North America by
FOUR COURTS PRESS
c/o ISBS, 920 N.E. 58th Avenue, Suite 300, Portland, OR 97213.

© Brian Griffin 2005

A catalogue record for this title
is available from the British Library.

ISBN 1–85182–950–4 hbk
ISBN 1–85182–821–4 pbk

All rights reserved. No part of this publication may be
reproduced, stored in or introduced into a retrieval system, or transmitted, in
any form or by any means (electronic, mechanical, photocopying, recording
or otherwise), without the prior written permission of both the copyright
owner and publisher of this book.

Printed in England
by Antony Rowe Ltd, Chippenham, Wilts.

Contents

List of illustrations 7

Preface 9

1 Historians on crime in Ireland, 1801–1921 11

2 Primary sources for the study of crime 18

Conclusion 91

Select bibliography 93

Illustrations

1 Detail of a page from Richard Hayes (ed.), *Manuscript sources for the history of Irish civilisation* (Boston, 1964).   19

2 Extract from Sir Francis B. Head, *Fortnight in Ireland* (London, 1852).   22

3 Extract from Adam Brockie's appeal to the lord lieutenant for clemency for his son, Criminal Index Files, CIF 1895/B18 (courtesy of the National Archives, Ireland).   32

4 Extract from *Report from the select committee on outrages (Ireland)* … HC 1852 (438) xiv 1.   51

5 Extract from *Return of judicial statistics of Ireland, 1863* HC 1864 [3418] lvii 653.   63

6 Extract from W. Steuart Trench, *Realities of Irish life* (London, 1868).   72

Preface

The study of crime, particularly the various agrarian disturbances of nineteenth-century Ireland and the violence of the War of Independence years, has been one of the most productive subjects for historians of the Union period in recent decades. What follows is a guide to the more useful secondary and primary sources for the researcher interested in building on what has already been published in this flourishing field of study. In this guide the definition of crime adopted is that of illegal activity as defined by contemporary laws. No moral judgment is to be inferred on the part of the author when examining popular agrarian outbreaks, Fenianism or the early twentieth-century separatist movement in this work: according to the law of the land, cattle-houghers, Fenian rebels and members of IRA flying columns were lawbreakers, hence the discussion of sources that are relevant to the study of such individuals in this guide.

The first chapter gives a brief overview of the main findings of historians' work on crime and disorder in Ireland during the Union period, with a view to helping researchers place their particular subject of interest in historiographical context. Chapter two surveys the principal primary sources available to the researcher, signalling the strengths and weaknesses of this material. In the final section, the main conclusions about sources for the study of crime are highlighted and suggestions are also made as to potentially rewarding areas of further research.

I would like to offer my thanks to the staff of the following institutions for their help in making this publication possible: the National Archives and the National Library of Ireland, the Public Record Office of Northern Ireland, the National Archives, Kew, the Archives Department of University College Dublin, the Bureau of Military History, the British Library, Trinity College Dublin library, and the library of Bath Spa University College. My colleagues in the History Department at Bath Spa University College, especially John Newsinger and Graham Davis, deserve a special mention for their support. I am grateful to Dr Mary Ann Lyons for asking me to write this guide, and for her painstaking editorial efforts.

My final word of thanks goes to my wife, Sally, for putting up with me when my mind was so often in the past instead of the present. This guide could not have been written without her unfailing encouragement and support.

CHAPTER I

Historians on crime in Ireland, 1801–1921

In the first decades of the nineteenth century, the maintenance of law and order was probably the principal preoccupation of the Dublin Castle authorities. The Union period, from their perspective, did not begin auspiciously. In parts of the country a state of low-intensity warfare was evident for a number of years, as the remnants of the United Irish organisation either conducted an intermittent guerilla campaign that sometimes involved brigandage, or engaged in conspiracy that eventually led to rebellion in 1803.[1] Although the United Irish threat proved to be ephemeral, the same could not be said of the challenge posed by the numerous outbreaks of agrarian outrage and disturbance in various parts of the country in the pre-Famine period. One baffled contemporary, commenting on the seeming ubiquity and protean nature of agrarian unrest, wrote in 1822 that 'it is difficult, if not impossible to ascertain the precise period of the first display or periodical return of the insurrectionary spirit, in consequence of the multifarious appellations and pretexts under which the disaffected have associated together'.[2] A similar state of confusion, or at least disagreement, over the nature of agrarian crime in pre-Famine Ireland may be said to exist among Irish historians. This disagreement has arisen from historians' differing interpretations of the contemporary evidence discussed in the guide below.

It was not always thus. Until recent decades, historians' perceptions of early nineteenth-century Irish agrarian crime were influenced by the analysis offered by the contemporary observer, George Cornewall Lewis. Lewis used the common contemporary term of Whiteboyism as a generic description of the various agrarian combinations of the period. He argued that

> The Whiteboy association may be considered as a vast trades' union for the protection of the Irish peasantry: the object being, not to regulate the rate of wages, or the hours of work, but to keep the actual occupant in possession of his land, and in general to regulate the relation of landlord and tenant for the benefit of the latter.[3]

---

[1] Marianne Elliott, *Partners in Revolution: the United Irishmen and France* (London and New Haven, 1982); Ruán O'Donnell, *Aftermath: post-rebellion insurgency in Wicklow, 1799–1803* (Dublin, 2000); Daniel J. Gahan, 'The "Black Mob" and the "Babes in the Wood": Wexford in the wake of rebellion, 1798–1806' in *Journal of the Wexford Historical Society*, 13 (1990–1), pp 92–110; Liam Chambers, *Rebellion in Kildare, 1790–1803* (Dublin, 1998), pp 103–20; idem, 'The State Solicitor's report on the 1803 rebellion in Kildare' in *Journal of the County Kildare Archaeological Society*, xix, part 1 (2000–01), pp 217–26. [2] Anonymous, *Historical sketches of the several rebellions, disturbances, and illegal associations in Ireland, from the earliest period to the year 1822* (Dublin, 1822), pp 49–50. [3] George Cornewall Lewis, *On local disturbances*

Lewis went on to state that

> Certain other objects are occasionally added, the chief of which is to prevent the employment of a stranger, the quantity of work being, in the opinion of the labourers, already insufficient for the natives: at times, moreover, the Whiteboys... have sought to reduce the rate of tithe, or to prevent its collection, or to lower the priests' dues. These combinations being constantly in existence, and working with weapons which may be turned to any purpose, the objects have become somewhat varied, but in general have been restricted simply to the occupation of land and the several payments immediately connected with it.[4]

While Lewis recognised, then, that agrarian disturbance involved more than tenants committing violent acts to defend their interests against landlords, and that labourers were also perpetrators of agrarian crime, he emphasised the notion of a tenants' defensive 'trades union' against landlords as the best means of understanding what Whiteboyism involved.

This remained, either implicitly or explicitly, the prevailing view of the issues involved in agrarian crime[5] until Joseph Lee's seminal 1973 article, 'The Ribbonmen'. Lee argued that most agrarian crime in pre-Famine Ireland arose from disputes between labourers and cottiers on one side and farmers on the other, rather than from disputes between farmers and landlords. A desire to control conacre rents and reduce potato prices accounted for most attacks on farmers, in his estimation.[6] Lee's article has prompted historians to pay more attention to the structure of Irish rural society, and particularly to tensions between and within the different strata below that of the landowners, in their efforts to explain the nature of agrarian crime. Thus Michael Beames, in his study of agrarian assassination in Tipperary between 1837 and 1847, explored a range of factors such as the class of the victims, the motives behind the crimes, the timing of the assassinations (most occurred between October and January, slack periods for peasant farmers and labourers) and the identity and class of the assassins, where known. This indicates the influence of Lee's approach in his 1973 article, although Beames concludes that Lee's explanation of the causes of agrarian crime as involving a struggle between cottiers and labourers and farmers over conacre rents and potato prices is inadequate and that, in fact, Lewis's characterisation of rural unrest as a defensive struggle of small tenant farmers against landlords is the more accurate. In Beames's study, it is the 'improving' or consolidating landlords and their agents who were the main assassination victims in Tipperary in this period, and tenant farmers, and some labourers, the main assassins.[7]

---

in Ireland; and on the Irish Church question (London, 1836), p. 99. **4** Ibid. **5** See John Pomfret, *The struggle for land in Ireland, 1800–1923* (Princeton, 1930). **6** Joseph Lee, 'The Ribbonmen' in T. Desmond Williams (ed.), *Secret societies in Ireland* (Dublin, 1973), pp 26–35. **7** M.R. Beames, 'Rural conflict in pre-Famine Tipperary: peasant assassinations in Tipperary, 1837–1847' in *Past & Present*, no. 81 (1978),

Support for Lee's broad interpretation comes in Paul Roberts's examination of the clashes between the Caravats and Shanavests in eleven counties from 1806 to 1811.[8] According to Roberts, the bloody and frequently murderous struggle between these factions was 'a novel extension of the struggle between the Whiteboys and the rural middle class, and its unique scale and violence reflected its roots in the supra-local and bitter loyalties of class'. The Caravats were 'primarily a Whiteboy organization', a 'kind of primitive syndicalist movement whose aim was apparently to absorb as many of the poor as possible into a network of autonomous local gangs, each exercising thoroughgoing control over its local economy, and the whole adding up to a generalized alternative system'. In contrast, the Shanavests were 'an unprecedented middle-class anti-Whiteboy movement formed specifically to combat the Caravats', and were composed principally of better-off farmers. While both factions came together to fight each other at fairs and other public gatherings, the Caravats also pursued a range of grievances that affected the less well-off sections of rural society, such as attempting to forcibly reduce food prices and rents, and the Shanavests acted as an anti-Whiteboy vigilante group.[9] Samuel Clark also argues that collective violence in the pre-Famine period mostly arose from hostility between large farmers and the 'rural poor', with most instances of violent crime being directed against the former and most demands made by 'violent gangs' reflecting the interests of the latter.[10] James S. Donnelly, while paying due attention to the social composition of those involved in committing agrarian crime and analysing their grievances and stated aims, modifies the views of Lee, Beames and Roberts. His study of the Carder and Caravat outbreaks from 1813 to 1816 in many parts of Munster and Leinster suggests that one-dimensional explanations of agrarian combinations do not fully explain the complexity of these movements. According to Donnelly, agrarian combinations that arose during times of agricultural prosperity, when farm prices were buoyant and land values were rising sharply, were usually dominated by the landless and those with little land: their aims were to restrain the inflation of conacre rents and food prices, to boost wages and frustrate the land-acquisitive ten-

---

pp 75–91; idem, *Peasants and power: the Whiteboy movements and their control in pre-Famine Ireland* (Brighton and New York, 1983). See also David Ryan, '"Ribbonism" and agrarian violence in County Galway, 1819–1820' in *Journal of the Galway Archaeological and Historical Society*, 52 (2000), pp 120–34, in which it is argued that the Ribbon outbreak of those years was triggered by 'unfavourable economic conditions' in the aftermath of the Napoleonic Wars and 'the maltreatment of the poor by landlords, middlemen and tithe-proctors'. **8** Paul E.W. Roberts, 'Caravats and Shanavests: Whiteboyism and faction fighting in East Munster, 1802–11' in Samuel Clark and James S. Donnelly, jr (eds), *Irish peasants: violence and political unrest, 1780–1914* (Madison and Manchester, 1983), pp 64–101. The counties affected were Tipperary, Waterford, Kilkenny, Limerick, Cork, Clare, Kerry, Queen's County, Carlow, Kildare and Wexford. **9** Ibid. For other discussions of factions in this period see Sailbheastar Ó Muireadhaigh, 'Na Carabhait agus na Sean-Bheisteanna' in *Galvia*, viii (1961), pp 4–20; Patrick O'Donnell, *The Irish faction fighters of the 19th century* (Dublin, 1975); James S. Donnelly, jr, 'Factions in pre-Famine Ireland' in Audrey S. Eyler and Robert F. Garratt (eds), *The uses of the past: essays on Irish culture* (Newark, 1988), pp 113–30. **10** Samuel Clark, 'The importance of agrarian classes: agrarian class structure and collective action in nineteenth-century Ireland' in *British Journal of Sociology*, 29, no. 1 (Mar. 1978), pp 22–40.

dencies of large farmers and graziers. However, agrarian combinations that arose as a result of a drastic decline in agricultural prices were generally marked by a progressive widening in their social composition, with relatively poor and relatively comfortable members of the rural community involved in the commission of agrarian crime.[11] David Fitzpatrick's study of agrarian crime in a single civil parish, that of Cloone in County Leitrim, offers an alternative to the preceding historians' arguments. Fitzpatrick contends that illegal collective action in rural areas that were apparently between classes may often be interpreted as struggles between families, and conflicts that are apparently within classes may be construed as struggles between rival family factions.[12]

While there is disagreement among these historians as to the social composition and motivation of various illegal agrarian combinations in the pre-Famine period, they all share the common desire of trying to understand and explain what the contemporary evidence tells us about the origins and nature of agrarian crime, by paying particular attention to the socio-economic context in which these crimes were committed.[13] A similar approach is evident in interpretations of the Land War of the 1879–1882 period, although, once again, there is no consensus among historians about why the Land War occurred and what it involved – in other words, they disagree as to what prompted the perpetrators of agrarian crime in breaking the law. The traditional view was that the Land War was the result of an explosion among tenant farmers ground down by predatory, rack-renting and evicting landlords, a view that was at least partly influenced by Land League propaganda about the issues at stake in the period.[14] More recent research has challenged this interpretation. Firstly, investigations by Barbara Solow and W.E. Vaughan have shown that, rather than post-Famine landlord-tenant relations being characterised by high rents and eviction rates on the one hand, and defensive agrarian outrages on the other, the reality was that down to the late 1870s rents failed to keep pace with price rises. In other words, tenant farmers, rather than landlords, were the 'winners' in Ireland's improving economic conditions after the Famine, and evictions and outrages were relatively rare.[15] James S. Donnelly has suggested that the origins of the

---

11 James S. Donnelly, jr, 'The social composition of agrarian rebellions in early nineteenth-century Ireland: the case of the Carders and Caravats, 1813–16' in Patrick J. Corish (ed.), *Radicals, rebels and establishments* (Belfast, 1985), pp 151–69. **12** David Fitzpatrick, 'Class, family and agrarian unrest in nineteenth-century Ireland' in P.J. Drudy (ed.), *Irish Studies 2: Ireland: land, politics and people* (Cambridge, 1982), pp 37–75. **13** See also John William Knott, 'Land, kinship and identity: the cultural roots of agrarian agitation in eighteenth- and nineteenth-century Ireland' in *The Journal of Peasant Studies*, xii, no. 1 (1984), pp 93–108; Gale E. Christianson, 'Secret societies and agrarian violence in Ireland, 1790–1840' in *Agricultural History*, 46 (July 1972), pp 369–84; James S. Donnelly, jr, 'The Terry Alt movement, 1829–31' in *History Ireland*, 2, no. 4 (winter 1994), pp 30–35; Maurice B. Kiely and William Nolan, 'Politics, land and rural conflict in County Waterford, c.1830–1845' in William Nolan and Thomas P. Power (eds), *Waterford history and society: interdisciplinary essays on the history of an Irish county* (Dublin, 1992), pp 459–94; Robert James Scally, *The end of hidden Ireland: rebellion, famine, and emigration* (Oxford, 1995); Kevin Kenny, *Making sense of the Molly Maguires* (Oxford, 1998). **14** Pomfret, *Struggle for land in Ireland*; N.D. Palmer, *The Irish Land League crisis* (New Haven, 1940). **15** Barbara Lewis Solow, *The land question and the Irish economy, 1870–1903* (Cambridge, Mass., 1971); W.E. Vaughan,

Land War are not to be found in the poverty of Irish tenant farmers, but in their relative prosperity: he posits that the agrarian crime and other disturbances in the late 1870s and early 1880s resulted from 'a revolution of rising expectations' on the part of these farmers. The downturn in the agricultural economy during this period was crucial in triggering the Land War, which should be viewed as a defence of the economic gains made by tenant farmers in the post-Famine era.[16] Samuel Clark and Paul Bew also focus on the agricultural depression as a causal factor, but come to differing conclusions as to what the Land War involved. Clark stresses the unity of interests and action of the tenant farming community in the period, a unity made easier by the structural and land-use changes in post-Famine rural society which led to the decreasing importance of the labouring and cottier classes.[17] According to Clark, the aims of the Land League were set and the rhetoric of the movement was produced to a relatively large extent by townsmen, who helped tenant farmers present a relatively united front against landlords. Townsmen, particularly traders in towns and villages – to whom tenant farmers were in debt – formed a disproportionately large segment of Land League membership and leadership, and were also over-represented in the number of suspects arrested under the Protection of Person and Property (Ireland) Act of 1881. Traders in towns, then, had a vested interest in discouraging their debtor farmer customers from paying landlords at their expense, which Clark suggests is an important factor in explaining the militancy of the agrarian agitation of this period.[18] Bew contests the thesis of the Land War representing the concerted action of a relatively united tenant-farming community. He argues that during the Land War, the Land League shifted from articulating the interests of the relatively impoverished small tenant farmers of the West to adopting aims that favoured the interests of the better-off farmers of Leinster and Munster, including graziers.[19] These differing interpretations illustrate the importance of local studies for understanding the nature of the Land War. More studies of agrarian crime and other forms of collective action – for instance, preventing landlords from pursuing their favourite activity of hunting or organising 'people's hunts'[20] – at the level

---

'Landlord and tenant relationships in Ireland between the Famine and the Land War, 1850–1870' in L.M. Cullen and T.C. Smout (eds), *Comparative aspects of Scottish and Irish economic and social history, 1600–1900* (Edinburgh, 1977), pp 216–26; idem, 'Agricultural output, rents and wages in Ireland, 1850–80' in L.M. Cullen and F. Furet (eds), *Ireland and France, 17th–20th centuries: towards a comparative study of rural history* (Paris, 1980), pp 85–97; idem, 'An assessment of the economic performance of Irish landlords, 1851–81' in F.S.L. Lyons and R.A.J. Hawkins (eds), *Ireland under the Union: varieties of tension: essays in honour of T.W. Moody* (Oxford, 1980), pp 173–79; idem, *Landlords and tenants in Ireland, 1848–1904* (Dundalk, 1984); idem, *Landlords and tenants in mid-Victorian Ireland* (Oxford, 1994). **16** James S. Donnelly, jr, *The land and the people of nineteenth-century Cork: the rural economy and the land question* (London, 1975). **17** On this topic see David Fitzpatrick, 'The disappearance of the Irish agricultural labourer, 1841–1912' in *Irish Economic and Social History*, vii (1980), pp 66–92. **18** Samuel Clark, 'The social composition of the Land League' in *Irish Historical Studies*, xvii, no. 68 (Sept 1971), pp 447–69; idem, *Social origins of the Irish Land War* (Princeton, 1979). **19** Paul Bew, *Land and the national question in Ireland, 1858–82* (Dublin, 1978). **20** L.P. Curtis, jr, 'Stopping the hunt, 1881–1882: an aspect of the Irish Land War' in C.E.H. Philbin (ed.), *Nationalism and popular protest in Ireland* (Cambridge, 1987), pp 349–402.

of the parish, barony or county are needed before a fuller picture emerges of the motives behind agrarian crime and disorder in Ireland in this period, and the generalisations of historians about the Land War at the national level are tested.[21]

Some progress has also been made in investigating the violence of the 1916–21 period at local level, but more local studies are needed. David Fitzpatrick, *Politics and Irish life, 1913–1921: provincial experience of war and revolution* (Dublin, 1977), an exhaustive examination of the struggle between Irish republicans and the forces of the Crown and their supporters in Clare, pioneered this microcosmic approach. Other useful examples are Oliver Coogan, *Politics and war in Meath, 1913–23* (Dublin, 1983), Peter Hart's impressive *The IRA and its enemies: violence and community in Cork, 1916–1923* (Oxford, 1998) and Marie Coleman, *County Longford and the Irish Revolution, 1912–1923* (Dublin, 2003). These comprehensive studies have been supplemented by numerous articles that investigate the activity of the IRA at county or town level[22] or that provide scholarly reappraisals of single incidents during the struggle for independence, such as the Ashbourne ambush in 1916.[23] The general picture that emerges from these works is that although the War of Independence was portrayed by Republicans as a war of national liberation, the IRA's military operations were, for the most part, conducted within a relatively limited geographical area. Most military actions by the IRA were disproportionately concentrated in a few distinct regions: Dublin and southern and central Munster in particular, with a smaller campaign in the southern Ulster and northern Leinster region. Even within the militarily more active counties, distinct geographic patterns of involvement in the struggle were evident. Some sections of the Catholic community were more involved than others, and rivalries between local IRA units and commanders, rather than propagating the war against the British, often seemed uppermost in activists' minds.[24] More investigations of the actions and motivation of IRA Volunteers[25] at

---

21 See Thomas Nelson, *The Land War in County Kildare* (Maynooth, 1985); Donald M. Jordan, 'Merchants, "strong farmers" and Fenians: the post-Famine political élite and the Irish Land War' in Philbin (ed.), *Nationalism and popular protest*, pp 320–48 (a study of the Land War in Mayo); idem, *Land and popular politics in Ireland: County Mayo from the plantation to the Land War* (Cambridge, 1994); J.W.H. Carter, *The Land War and its leaders in Queen's County, 1879–82* (Portlaoise, 1994); Margaret Urwin, *A County Wexford family in the Land War: the O'Hanlon Walshs of Knocktartan* (Dublin, 2002). For a good general discussion see Joseph Lee, 'The Land War' in Liam de Paor (ed.), *Milestones in Irish history* (Cork and Dublin, 1986), pp 106–16. 22 Dermot Francis, 'Derry and the 1916 Easter Rising' in *Ulster Folklife*, xxxviii (1992), pp 34–46; Maria Boyne, 'The War of Independence in Trim, 1919–21' in Liam McNiffe (ed.), *Meath: studies in local history* (Navan, n.d.), pp 173–81; Peter Hart, 'Class, community and the Irish Republican Army in Cork, 1917–1923' in Patrick O'Flanagan and Cornelius G. Buttimer (eds), *Cork history and society: interdisciplinary essays on the history of an Irish county* (Dublin, 1993), pp 963–85; Joost Augusteijn, 'Radical nationalist activities in County Derry, 1900–1921' in Gerard O'Brien (ed.), *Derry and Londonderry history and society: interdisciplinary essays on the history of an Irish county* (Dublin, 1999), pp 573–600. 23 Terence M. Dooley, 'Alexander "Baby" Gray (1858–1916) and the battle at Ashbourne, 28 April 1916' in *Ríocht na Mídhe*, xiv (2003), pp 194–229. 24 For general discussions on the War of Independence see Charles Townshend, *Political violence in Ireland: government and resistance since 1848* (Oxford, 1983); Joost Augusteijn, *From public defiance to guerilla warfare: the experience of ordinary volunteers in the Irish War of Independence, 1916–1921* (Dublin, 1996). 25 Joost Augusteijn,

local level will enable one to come to a more informed assessment of this violent phase in Ireland's history.

Thus far, this introductory overview to the literature on crime, disorder and political violence in Ireland has focused on agrarian crime and the violence of the 1916–1921 period. While this reflects the main interests of historians who are or have been studying illegal activities during the Union period, the researcher should also be aware that other topics have engaged the interest of Irish historians.[26] No literature overview would be complete without mentioning Angela Bourke's *The burning of Bridget Cleary: a true story* (London, 1999). This examination of the notorious killing of a 26-year-old Tipperary woman by her relatives in 1895 builds on anthropological research and folklore studies to offer a unique insight into the minds of the perpetrators, and it illustrates vividly the value of the local study to the historian of crime in Ireland.[27]

The following chapter – the main part of this guide – introduces researchers to the principal primary sources for the local study of crime in Ireland. It is subdivided into sections that discuss manuscripts, parliamentary papers, diaries, memoirs and travellers' accounts, published proceedings of trials and newspapers, respectively.

'Motivation: Why did they fight for Ireland? The motivation of volunteers in the revolution' in Joost Augusteijn (ed.), *The Irish revolution, 1913–1923* (Basingstoke and New York, 2002), pp 103–20. **26** See for example Pauline M. Prior, 'Mad, not bad: crime, mental disorder and gender in nineteenth-century Ireland' in *History of Psychiatry*, viii (1997), pp 501–16; Caitríona Clear, 'Homelessness, crime, punishment and poor relief in Galway, 1850–1914: an introduction' in *Journal of the Galway Archaeological and Historical Society*, 50 (1998), pp 118–34. **27** For an examination of another *cause célèbre* in this period see James Carney, *The playboy and the yellow lady* (Dublin, 1986), a discussion of the case of James Lynchehaun.

CHAPTER 2

Primary sources for the study of crime

This chapter aims to introduce the reader to the principal primary sources for the study of Irish crime. As well as indicating the location and general content of this material, it offers comments on the usefulness and shortcomings of the respective primary sources. The order in which they are discussed below is not intended as a reflection of their relative importance to the researcher. Such considerations as the topic of research, the time period and geographical focus of the study will determine the choice of source to be consulted. Almost certainly, more than one of the types of primary source discussed in the chapter below will be of interest and use to the researcher.

MANUSCRIPT SOURCES

There are very few published guides to manuscript sources for the study of crime. The best is Richard Hayes (ed.), *Manuscript sources for the history of Irish civilisation* (12 vols, Boston, 1964) and *Manuscript sources for the history of Irish civilisation: first supplement* (3 vols, Boston, 1979).[1] Maria Luddy, Catherine Cox, Leeann Land and Diane Urquhart's CD-ROM and internet database, *A directory of sources for women's history in Ireland*, produced by the Women's History Project, constitutes an easy-to-use finding aid for researchers with a particular interest in women and crime.[2] Those researching the history of the Land War will find Fergus Campbell's brief guide to manuscript source material of considerable value.[3] The researcher into the history of crime is also advised to consult the bibliographies of secondary sources, as these can offer invaluable guidance on the type and location of material that is available. A particularly good example is the annotated bibliography in David Fitzpatrick's *Politics and Irish life*. There are also a number of useful published collections of facsimile documents that one may find useful as a quick guide to some of the types of manuscript material that are available. These include *Transportation Ireland-Australia, 1798–1848* (Dublin, 1983), a selection of facsimile documents that throw light on the categories of offences for which convicts were transported in the first half of the

---

1 Researchers should note that the references to the State Paper Office and Public Record Office should now read as references to the National Archives, Dublin.   2 The database may be accessed at http://www.nationalarchives.ie/wh/sources.html   3 Fergus Campbell, 'The hidden history of the Irish Land War: a guide to local sources' in Carla King (ed.), *Famine, land and culture in Ireland* (Dublin, 2000), pp 140–53.

1 Detail of a page from Richard Hayes (ed.), *Manuscript sources for the history of Irish civilisation* (Boston, 1964).

nineteenth century,[4] and the National Library of Ireland's collection, *The Land War, 1879–1903* (Dublin, 1976).

SOURCES IN THE NATIONAL ARCHIVES OF IRELAND

The National Archives of Ireland[5] is by far the most important repository for the student wishing to research the history of crime in Ireland. Before describing the rich potential of its sources, a brief overview of the machinery of law and order in nineteenth-century Ireland is necessary.

During the Union period the Irish executive was headed by the lord lieutenant. He was assisted by a chief secretary who, in turn, was assisted by an under-secretary.[6] Although the lord lieutenant was nominally in charge of the executive, most of the day-to-day running of the Irish administration was overseen by the chief secretary.[7] A vast amount of correspondence was dealt with by the Chief Secretary's Office in Dublin Castle on a daily basis, much of which concerned the maintenance of law and order. All major questions relating to the operation, discipline and distribution of the two police forces controlled by Dublin Castle were referred to the Chief Secretary's Office. It also supervised the stipendiary or resident magistrates, corresponded with the unpaid justices of the peace, handled all questions regarding the relations of the civil and military power, received memorials from prisoners and convicts, and transmitted the orders of the attorney general (who was the director of criminal prosecutions) to the police and crown solicitors concerned.[8]

The Chief Secretary's Office has, understandably, been described as 'the mainspring of the Irish administration' under the Union.[9] As stated above, much of its

---

4 These documents were originally stored in the State Paper Office, and are now stored in the National Archives, Dublin.   **5** National Archives, Bishop Street, Dublin 8.   **6** For an overview of the Irish executive under the Union see R.B. McDowell, 'The Irish executive in the nineteenth century' in *Irish Historical Studies*, ix, no. 35 (1955), pp 264–80 and idem, *The Irish administration, 1801–1914* (London, 1964).   **7** For a general study of Dublin Castle's approach to law and order during the Union period see Virginia Crossman, *Politics, law and order in nineteenth-century Ireland* (Dublin, 1996). For general examinations of the executive's law and order policies for shorter periods see Brian Jenkins, 'The chief secretary' in D.G. Boyce and Alan O'Day (eds), *Defenders of the Union: a survey of British and Irish unionism since 1801* (New York and London, 2001), pp 39–64 (a study of the chief secretaryships of William Wellesley-Pole, Robert Peel and Henry Goulburn); L.P. Curtis, jr, *Coercion and conciliation in Ireland, 1880–1892: a study in Conservative Unionism* (Princeton, 1963); Margaret O'Callaghan, *British high politics and a nationalist Ireland: criminality, land and the law under Forster and Balfour* (Cork, 1994); Eunan O'Halpin, *The decline of the Union: British government in Ireland, 1892–1920* (Dublin, 1987). There are also a number of important studies of individual chief secretaries and under-secretaries: Brian Jenkins, *Henry Goulburn, 1784–1856: a political biography* (Liverpool, 1996), pp 130–84; Gearóid Ó Tuathaigh, *Thomas Drummond and the government of Ireland, 1835–41* (Dublin, 1979); Catherine B. Shannon, *Arthur Balfour and Ireland, 1874–1922* (Cork, 1988); Leon Ó Broin, *The chief secretary: Augustine Birrell and Ireland, 1907–16* (London, 1969); D.G. Boyce and Cameron Hazlehurst, 'The unknown chief secretary: H.E. Duke and Ireland, 1916–18' in *Irish Historical Studies*, xx, no. 79 (March 1977), pp 286–311. The chief secretaries are listed in J.L.J. Hughes, 'The chief secretaries in Ireland, 1566–1921' in *Irish Historical Studies*, viii, no. 29 (Mar. 1952), pp 59–72.   **8** McDowell, *Irish administration*, pp 71–2.   **9** Ibid., p.71.

personnel's time was taken up with overseeing the operations of the two principal police forces of nineteenth-century Ireland. The first was the Royal Irish Constabulary (RIC), established in 1822 as a county constabulary with provincial inspectors general, and reformed as the uniform Irish Constabulary in 1836 under the command of a single inspector-general. The force received the epithet 'Royal' in recognition of its services in suppressing the Fenian rebellion in 1867. The second was the Dublin Metropolitan Police force (DMP), which was under the supervision of the Chief Secretary's Office from 1838. Between 1814 and 1836 another police unit, the Peace Preservation Force, was also directed by Dublin Castle; as part of a major reform of Irish policing in 1836, this latter force was abolished and most of its members were recruited into the Irish Constabulary. From early in the Union period, then, Ireland was the most heavily policed part of the United Kingdom. The constabulary, who were stationed in some 1,594 barracks scattered throughout Ireland in 1852,[10] had an intimate knowledge of the localities in which they were stationed. Their ubiquity was aptly summed up by a Canadian visitor:

> If a new lord-lieutenant in a very great hurry wished to obtain a correct general idea of the distribution of the constabulary force of Ireland – in case no poor little boy, with a face freckled or pitted with the small-pox, happened to be in the neighbourhood – I would strongly advise him to buy a sixpenny map of Ireland, nail it to a tree, and then, standing twenty-five yards from it, to fire at it with a close-carrying single-barrelled gun loaded with snipe-shot, which, in one second, would, as nearly as possible, mark out for him the distribution of the constabulary throughout the country he was about to govern.[11]

Another astute contemporary observer, recognising the importance of the constabulary's role at local level for the Dublin Castle authorities, claimed in 1881 that 'Everything in Ireland, from the muzzling of a dog to the suppression of a rebellion, is done by the Irish constabulary.'[12] Their reports, along with those of the DMP, constitute an essential source for the study of crime in the nineteenth and twentieth centuries. Most of the surviving police reports are housed in the National Archives.

Reports from magistrates, especially resident magistrates but also justices of the peace, are the other main sources for the study of crime that are held in the National Archives. Most cases involving breaches of the law consisted of non-indictable offences. From 1822 a nation-wide system of petty sessions was established, whereby these cases were tried before a bench of magistrates, most of whom were unpaid justices of the peace.[13] At the same time that the system of petty sessions was being

---

10 Sir Francis B. Head, *Fortnight in Ireland* (London, 1852), p. 43. **11** Ibid., p.42. **12** Henry Blake, 'The Irish police' in *Nineteenth Century*, ix (Feb. 1881), p. 390. **13** Ian Bridgeman, 'The constabulary and the criminal justice system in nineteenth-century Ireland' in *Criminal Justice History*, xv (1995), p. 100. For a study of the petty sessions in one county see Desmond McCabe, 'Magistrates, peasants and the petty sessions courts: Mayo, 1823–50' in *Cathair na Mart*, v (1985), pp 45–53. Richard McMahon,

2 Extract from Sir Francis B. Head, *Fortnight in Ireland* (London, 1852).

established, another reform of the legal system at the local level was instituted with the introduction of stipendiary or resident magistrates. The fact that they were salaried magistrates, and had no family connection with the people of the districts in which they adjudicated, was deemed by Dublin Castle to be a guarantee against the claims of partiality that were often levelled against justices of the peace in pre-Famine Ireland.[14] The number of resident magistrates fluctuated, with some 72 stationed in Ireland in 1860 and 64 in 1912;[15] whatever their numbers, they were regarded as the most important strand of the machinery of justice at the local level by the Dublin Castle authorities. Throughout the nineteenth and early twentieth centuries, the reports of magistrates and police form the single most important source for the study of crime and disorder in Ireland.[16]

(a) State of the Country Papers

For the researcher investigating crime and disorder in the first two decades of the nineteenth century, the State of the Country Papers, which date from the 1796–1831 period, are the principal source that one should consult. As the name of this collection suggests, the State of the Country Papers tend to focus on crimes that were deemed subversive of the public peace, such as faction fighting or, more commonly, agrarian crime. They have their origin in an earlier collection, the Rebellion Papers,[17] which documents the origins and progress of the United Irish movement, and the progress and aftermath of the 1798 Rebellion, including the insurrection of 1803. Nancy J. Curtin has pointed to one of the pitfalls in using such material, as it means that the historian's interpretation 'must be filtered through the lens of magistrates, office-holders, and informers',[18] the principal originators of the reports that form the bulk of the Rebellion Papers and the State of the Country Papers. One rarely reads, at first hand, about the motives of the perpetrators of crime or the opinions of suspects in official records. The best that one can usually expect is to read threatening letters or notices, or second-hand, reported accounts of the words and actions of lawbreakers and suspected lawbreakers. The State of the Country Papers frequently reflect the anxious state of mind of magistrates, yeomanry officers, policemen, mem-

---

'The regional administration of a central legal policy' in Leon Litvack and Glenn Hooper (eds), *Ireland in the nineteenth century: regional identity* (Dublin, 2000), pp 156–68 studies the operation of the petty sessions at Gurteen, County Galway, in the late 1830s. **14** Galen Broeker, *Rural disorder and police reform in Ireland, 1812–1836* (London, 1970). **15** R.B. McDowell, 'The Irish courts of law, 1801–1914' in *Irish Historical Studies*, x (1956–57), p. 374. **16** For a brief account of such material relating to Ulster see Peter Collins, *Pathways to Ulster's past: sources and resources for local studies* (Belfast, 1998), pp 53–4. For the history of the resident magistrates see Penny Bonsall, *The Irish RMs: the resident magistrates in the British administration of Ireland* (Dublin, 1997). **17** For a discussion of the Rebellion Papers and the origin of the Outrage Papers see L.M. Cullen, 'Politics and rebellion: Wicklow in the 1790s' in Ken Hannigan and William Nolan (eds), *Wicklow history and society: interdisciplinary essays on an Irish county* (Dublin, 1994), pp 411–17; Deirdre Lindsay, 'The Rebellion Papers: an introduction to the Rebellion Papers collection in the National Archives, Bishop Street, Dublin' in *Ulster Local Studies*, 18, no. 2 (spring 1997), pp 28–42; idem, 'The Rebellion Papers' in *History Ireland*, 6, no. 2 (summer 1998), pp 18–22. **18** Nancy J. Curtin, *The United Irishmen: popular politics in Ulster and Dublin, 1791–1798* (Oxford, 1994), p. 3.

bers of the gentry and other loyalists concerning the possibility of another major rebellion. This accounts for the fact that the collection often contains reports of innocuous assemblies of country people, meetings that the authorities viewed with suspicion as possibly heralding something more sinister, such as the reports on the crowds who assembled for a hurling match in Galway in 1804, stable boys who assembled for a similar reason at the Curragh, County Kildare, in 1807, or the crowd who assembled for a pattern at Magheracloone, County Monaghan, in the same year.[19] Although the vigilance of the forces of law and order and their supporters led to reports that, on closer examination, do not deal with crime or disorder, even such false reports are not without interest to the historian as they shed light on the state of mind of police and other functionaries at local level. There is no doubt, however, that their vigilance also frequently resulted in invaluable information on the extent of real crime, or at least crime that was deemed subversive of public order. Crimes that could not be given a 'political' reading, such as pocket-picking or common larceny, do not feature in this body of material. Some reports in the State of the Country Papers are rather short, but the historian will also be rewarded with bulky documents when trawling through this material. A good example of a substantial body of papers relating to a single crime is the collection of police reports and witness depositions concerning the Wildgoose Lodge murders in Louth in 1816.[20]

The State of the Country Papers are catalogued in two calendars, one covering each of the years from 1796 to 1820 and the other covering each of the years from 1821 to 1831. The reports are not arranged by provinces or counties before 1808; those for 1808 to 1810 are partially arranged by provinces and counties, and from 1811 onwards this method of organising the material was the one that was systematically adopted. The latter arrangement makes the later material of especial value to the local historian, although he or she will also be able to find documents of relevance in the pre-1808 papers if the calendars are read with care. The best way to indicate the nature of this source is to concentrate on one county's reports for one year, in this instance, the reports from Meath in 1819.[21]

As the calendar shows, all of the Meath reports in 1819 are catalogued with the prefix SOC 2078. To procure individual reports for Meath for this year, one must use this prefix when ordering documents, and then add the relevant sub-number as indicated in the catalogue. For instance, SOC 2078/10 is a letter dated 9 April 1819 from George Brabazon, a magistrate and the vicar of Clonard, to Under-sec-

---

19 State of the Country Papers (hereafter SOC) 1026/17, SOC 1120/30, SOC 1120/59. **20** SOC 1828/15. For discussions of the Wildgoose Lodge murders see T.G.F. Patterson, 'The burning of Wildgoose Lodge' in *Journal of the County Louth Archaeological and Historical Society*, 12, no. 2 (1950), pp 159–80; Daniel J. Casey, 'Carleton in Louth' in *Journal of the County Louth Archaeological and Historical Society*, 17, no. 2 (1970), pp 97–106; idem, 'Wildgoose Lodge: the evidence and the lore' in *Journal of the County Louth Archaeological and Historical Society*, 18, no. 2 (1974), pp 140–64; Réamonn Ó Muirí, 'The burning of Wildgoose Lodge: a selection of documents' in *Journal of the County Louth Archaeological and Historical Society*, 21, no. 2 (1986), pp 117–47. **21** One study of crime in Meath that relies heavily on the State of the Country Papers is Desmond Mooney, 'The origins of agrarian violence in Meath, 1790–1828' in *Ríocht na Midhe*, viii, no. 1 (1987), pp 45–67.

retary William Gregory. In the letter, Brabazon recounts how the badly decomposed body of an unknown man, presumed to have been murdered, has been found in a tunnel of the Royal Canal near his house. He also declares his belief that a man named Walsh, from the Hill of Down, in whose house 'the Ribbon men held their meetings last winter', was involved in the homicide. In SOC 2078/12, dated 14 April 1819, Brabazon reports that an inquest was held on the body of the man and that the investigations into the supposed murder revealed that he was probably a Mr Boardman, who came to reside in Clonard in January 1818, and who disappeared on 28 January 1818 after leaving his house to catch the boat to Dublin. He had £300 in his possession at the time, so presumably robbery was the motive for his killing. There are other incidental details in Brabazon's two letters, and additional reports from the Clonard region, that provide valuable evidence to a local historian about crime in this part of southern Meath at this period.

Most of the reports from Meath in 1819 come from the proclaimed south-western part of the county.[22] Villages such as Clonard, Killyon, Longwood, Rathmolyon and the surrounding districts feature prominently in these reports; while crime and disorder in other parts of the county are occasionally reported on, such reports are heavily outnumbered by those describing the state of affairs in the south-west. This highlights one of the salient features of the State of the Country Papers: only outrages, variously defined, tend to form the subject matter of their reports, and the historian is largely left in the dark as to the incidence of other kinds of crime in the same period and, indeed, in the same county.

The reports of outrages in Meath in 1819 vary in their subject matter and nature. Some consist of strident, but vague, reports of the existence of 'Ribbonism' in various localities or detail the general unwillingness of the peasantry to assist in apprehending the perpetrators of agrarian crime;[23] others provide detailed accounts of individual outrages. Examples of the latter include reports of the malicious burning of the house of Andrew Goulding of Longwood by a band led by 'Captain Fearnot & Captain Good Reason', despite the presence of a joint military and police patrol that was searching for an illicit still at the time of the arson attack, and the burning of a police officer's house in the same village;[24] the robbery of money and arms from farmers in Crowboy, and the levelling of ditches and fences and malicious stabbing of cattle in the same area;[25] the demolition at Trammond, by a band of around 100 men, of a house built by a Mr Edward Purdon on land from which a previous tenant had been evicted for rent;[26] and the murder of Michael Fegan at Kilglass, as he was returning home from a cock-fight at Longwood.[27]

Most of these reports originate from police officers or magistrates, although some of them are sworn depositions by witnesses (usually victims) of outrages. While

---

22 The proclaimed district contained the parishes of Killaconnigan, Clonard, Killyon and Rathmolyon. See SOC 2078/16. **23** SOC 2078/1, SOC 2078/8. **24** SOC 2078/1, SOC 2078/2, SOC 2078/5, SOC 2078/22, SOC 2078/23. Goulding had taken 'a small quantity' of disputed land near Longwood, and refused to hand over his arms to a band of between 60 and 100 men. **25** SOC 2078/4, SOC 2078/15, SOC 2078/25. **26** SOC 2078/1. **27** SOC 2078/21.

this information is undoubtedly valuable to the historian of crime, one should still be sceptical about the motives behind the filing of some reports and question the veracity of some of the details contained in them. Consider the following copy of an extract from a report by James Tandy, a magistrate and the most prolific writer of reports to Dublin Castle from the disturbed areas of Meath in this period. It describes his activities against nocturnal and early morning meetings of suspected crowds of the peasantry:

> I mentioned my having proceeded from my own house at two o'clock on that morn[in]g to Lesclogher near to Athboy on the borders of West Meath, in consequence of private information I had received the even[in]g before of an intended meeting of those deluded people. On my arrival at the dawn of day I found my information too correct – that after remonstrating with them on their folly & wickedness they retired with an assurance that they would not meet again, but on such promises as I predicted much relyance could not be placed.
>
> [T]hey kept their words till last Sunday week when a meeting was held at Ferain[?] near Athboy about four miles from the former place, & on Sunday last renewed, at sun rise, their numbers I understand from twelve to fifteen hundred. [T]heir meetings are held with such a degree of secrecy that altho in rather a populous neighbourhood, yet the inhabitants either pretend, or are ignorant on the subject. [I]t appeared the former meeting which I heard of by chance was their third in that quarter, when their numbers were upwards of two thousand & on the morn[in]g I was there from what I saw, I make no doubt would not have been less – and among them a description of people far beyond the lower order.
>
> [T]here has of late been several strangers in this part of the country, some I hear from Dublin affecting to have come with information from [illegible word]. Something deep and mysterious is certainly going forward, notwithstanding the appearant quiet of the country. [T]he manners of the people are more manfully altered within this last fortnight.
>
> I have no doubt that there are emissarys to raise the spirit of the disaffected at the same time, I do not apprehend at present anything serious. I was enabled by your assistance last winter & aspiring to disarm the great portion of those Ribbon Men, they have now changed their name to Nights of St. Patrick but their plans & system [remain] the same, [with] merely a new oath which is becoming general.
>
> There has also been several nightly meetings of their leaders, where it seems I have been denounced in strong terms, at one of those meetings a few nights since they had two regular sentinels placed to prevent surprise from 'bloody Tandy', a name they have thought proper to designate me with, but no threats of assassination shall ever deter nor prevent me from discharging my duty, whatever your wishes are, you have only to honor

me with them, & as far as man can go, you may always rely on him, who has the honor to remain
Dear Sir
with every respect & Esteem
your faithful & obliged humble serv[an]t
James Tandy.[28]

The problems with this source are obvious. Tandy's motive in writing this report was clearly, in part, a desire to curry favour with Dublin Castle by creating an impression of zeal in the performance of his duties. In doing so, he probably exaggerated the extent of the threat that he was countering, the nature of which remains nebulous from a reading of his report (if, indeed, a threat existed at all). It is impossible to assess the degree to which other magistrates, policemen and functionaries of the law behaved as Tandy did, creating reports which give a problematic description of crime and disorder in their respective districts, either by exaggerated or partial accounts or accounts that lack candour. Another report from Meath in 1819 illustrates some of the problems with which the researcher should be prepared to deal. On 17 September Magistrate William Walsh of Stedalt, near Gormanston, wrote the following to Sir William Gregory:

> I think it my duty as a magistrate to state to you for the information of government that a serious disturbance or general rising is daily expected by the lower orders in this county. No further particulars have been stated to me but the accounts I have receiv[e]d both verbally & by Letter from places far separated from each other all agree in this point. A confidential person yesterday morning told me this & said that a search for arms would take place immediately & a House was actually searched last night & robbed of some yeomanry Arms & other articles. A very well conducted Protestant constable residing in Duleek told me that all the drunken Fellows from that to Navan are muttering something relative to general revenge.
>
> I do not wish to be considered an Alarmist but I would think it a dereliction of my duty if I did not communicate to government the information I have received.

Gregory was blunt in his response to the chief secretary, Charles Grant, on 19 September:

> Mr Walsh is I believe what he does not think himself, a genuine Alarmist. Stedalt, his residence, is not 2 miles from Lord Gormanston's; and it is not probable that any serious evil could be meditated by the Catholic popula-

---

[28] SOC 2078/39: letter from James Tandy, Carn Isle, to Sir James Grant, 17 Oct. 1819. The spelling and most of the punctuation and use of capitals are as in the original; a number of commas have been replaced with full stops.

tion of that part [of the] country, which should be communicated to Mr Walsh, & of which Lord G[ormanston] is ignorant.[29]

Gregory's caution is a salutary example of the approach that the researcher should take when reading the State of the Country Papers. While they offer valuable insights into the state of crime and disorder in early nineteenth-century Ireland, they should not be taken at face value. Where possible, one should try to gain an alternative perspective on the events described in the State of the Country Papers from other contemporary sources, or at least be prepared to question their accounts, or aspects of them, as the case requires.

(b) The Outrage Papers

The Outrage Papers, which document the years from 1832 to 1850, are a separate body of material from the State of the Country Papers but their contents are in many ways similar to the files in the latter collection. The Outrage Papers focus almost exclusively on agrarian crimes or on collective violence and intimidation connected with the opposition to tithe payment,[30] and, like the earlier body of papers, they were penned mainly by magistrates and policemen. The only noteworthy difference between the two is that police reports constitute a higher proportion of the Outrage Papers than the State of the Country Papers, which reflects the constabulary's increased importance in the enforcement of law and order in rural Ireland by the 1830s. As with the State of the Country Papers, the Outrage Papers ignore lesser crimes, and the volume of material for a particular county depends on how disturbed that particular county was during the period that one has chosen to study. They certainly enable the researcher to gain a good view, from the perspective of the magistracy and police, of the causes and nature of serious crime, especially agrarian crime, at county level or more local level if a particular village or group of townlands experienced serious crimes in this period.[31] They can also provide the material for a detailed investigation of individual crimes, as John B. Cunningham shows in his study of the attempted murder of a Fermanagh landlord in October 1845.[32]

---

29 SOC 2078/34. **30** For accounts of the Tithe War that rely heavily on the Outrage Papers see Patrick O'Donoghue, 'Causes of the opposition to tithes, 1830–1838' in *Studia Hibernica*, no. 5 (1965), pp 7–28; idem, 'Opposition to tithe payment in 1830–31' in *Studia Hibernica*, no. 6 (1966), pp 69–98; idem, 'Opposition to tithe payment in 1832–33' in *Studia Hibernica*, no. 12 (1972), pp 77–108; Michael O'Hanrahan, 'The Tithe War in County Kilkenny, 1830–1834' in William Nolan and Kevin Whelan (eds), *Kilkenny history and society: interdisciplinary essays on the history of an Irish county* (Dublin, 1990), pp 481–505; Stephen Randolph Gibbons, 'Captain Rock in the Queen's County' in Pádraig G. Lane and William Lane (eds), *Laois history and society: interdisciplinary essays on the history of an Irish county* (Dublin, 1999), pp 487–512; Liam Ó Donnchadha, 'The murder of Rev. Charles Ferguson, 1832' in *Bandon Historical Journal*, no. 6 (1990), pp 3–9. **31** Desmond Mooney, 'A new order established: agrarian violence in Meath 1835–44' in *Ríocht na Midhe*, viii, no. 3 (1990–91), pp 118–33. **32** John B. Cunningham, 'The investigation into the attempted assassination of Folliott Warren Barton near Pettigo, on 31 October 1845' in *Clogher Record*, xiii, no. 3 (1990), pp 125–45.

(c) Registered papers of the Chief Secretary's Office

The Registered Papers of the Chief Secretary's Office constitute a source of immense potential for the historian of crime and disorder in Ireland. These files date from 1818 to 1924, filling some 3,770 cartons. They represent a veritable treasure-trove for the researcher, as they document virtually all aspects of the British administration of Ireland in the Union period, and the enforcement of law and order is one of the main subjects dealt with by this vast body of correspondence. The Registered Papers differ from the State of the Country Papers and the Outrage Papers in that, as well as containing reports of major crimes, they also document the incidence of a vast range of lesser offences, such as illicit distillation, common assault, drunkenness, vagrancy, poaching, allowing cattle to stray onto the public road and, from the early 1890s onwards, illegally cycling on footpaths: in short, the whole gamut of indictable and non-indictable offences form the subject matter of this unsurpassable resource for the historian of crime.

Gaining access to this material is, however, a complicated and frequently frustrating business. This is partly due to the process involved in identifying and ordering the documents that one wishes to consult. The system of registering incoming correspondence to the Chief Secretary's Office underwent a number of changes between 1818 and 1852, but remained constant from 1853 to 1924. Mastering the system of registration in the unwieldy 337 indexes and registers in the National Archives reading room takes patience and care, but is essential for the researcher who wishes to locate and examine specific Registered Papers. The researcher is advised to consult Tom Quinlan's excellent guide to the Registered Papers[33] as the best means of familiarising oneself with the process of identifying and ordering relevant files. Even when one has identified the documents that one wishes to consult, one should be prepared for a certain amount of frustration in using this material[34] as not all of the documents that one orders will still be extant.[35] Nevertheless, the process of identifying and ordering Registered Papers is worth persevering with, as even if only a fraction of the material that one orders is still extant, this should prove invaluable for studying the particular topic in which one is interested. The richness of the Registered Papers for the historian of crime is illustrated by the use made of them by Maura Murphy in her fascinating examination of the activities of singers of seditious ballads in nineteenth-century Ireland, for example, and also in

---

33 Tom Quinlan, 'The registered papers of the Chief Secretary's Office' in *Irish Archives* (autumn 1995), pp 5–21. There is also useful information in Marianne Cosgrave, Rena Lohan and Tom Quinlan, 'Sources in the National Archives for researching the Great Famine' in *Irish Archives* (spring 1995), pp 24–44.   **34** On this general note of frustration, the researcher should be aware that that the staff at the National Archives enquiry desk are not always aware of the material held in the repository, or they sometimes give unclear, contradictory or incorrect advice. In such cases, the researcher should request the help of one of the archivists, as they can invariably guide one on the right track.   **35** Personal experience suggests that a very large proportion of the registered papers has been lost. For instance, many registered papers went to make up Crown files at assizes and quarter sessions and most of these were lost in the destruction of the Four Courts in 1922.

Pádraig Lane's study of violent crimes committed by agricultural labourers in the post-Famine decades.[36] Two much smaller collections that are apparently related to the Registered Papers (to judge by their content, which does not seem to differ significantly from the latter collection) are the Official Papers which cover the period from 1790 to 1831, and the Official Papers Miscellaneous Assorted, spanning the years 1780 to 1882. There is a two-volume calendar to the former collection available for consultation in the National Archives reading room, while the finding aid to the latter collection is a bound, indexed descriptive list. Although most of the papers in these collections that touch on crime and policing matters deal with police administration, one can also locate papers whose subject matter is crime. The Registered Papers of the Chief Secretary's Office, however, are of vastly greater importance to the researcher than the latter two collections of papers.

(d) Prisoners' petitions

One of the main drawbacks associated with much of the National Archives of Ireland material relating to crime and disorder is that it is rarely generated by the perpetrators of crime or persons suspected of breaking the law. Most of the relevant documentation reflects the observations and opinions of various layers of officialdom, and the historian has to take this into account when assessing what this material says about crime at local level. There is, however, one type of source that enables the historian to hear from law-breakers in their own words about their motives or alleged motives for their transgressions: petitions of clemency to the lord lieutenant. These petitions – known as memorials – were drawn up by convicted prisoners or, on occasion, their relatives, and submitted to the lord lieutenant for his decision on whether to commute the sentence. They have provided a rich seam of source material for such works as George Rudé's *Protest and punishment: the story of the social and political protesters transported to Australia, 1788–1868* (Oxford, 1978), Portia Robinson's study of juvenile crime in pre-Famine Ireland, Shaun Byrne's examination of pre-Famine crime in Donegal, Brenda Mooney's exploration of female criminals and their crimes in Wexford and Waterford in the same period and Leonora Irwin's similar study for Dublin, Sinead Curley's research into the crimes committed by Clare prisoners who were transported in 1839–1840 and 1846–47, Elizabeth Steiner-Scott's investigation of domestic violence in post-Famine Ireland, and Frank Sweeney's account of the murder of Conell Boyle at Meendernasloe, Annagry, in 1898.[37]

36 Maura Murphy, 'The ballad singer and the role of the seditious ballad in nineteenth-century Ireland: Dublin Castle's view' in *Ulster Folklife*, 25 (1979), pp 79–102; Pádraig G. Lane, 'Agricultural labourers and rural violence, 1850–1914' in *Studia Hibernica*, no. 27 (1993), pp 77–87. **37** Portia Robinson, 'The desolate boys: juvenile crime and punishment, Ireland and New South Wales' in Oliver MacDonagh and W.F. Mandle (eds), *Ireland and Irish-Australia: studies in cultural and political history* (London, Sydney and Wolfeboro, 1986), pp 229–47; Shaun Byrne, '"The law must take its course": crime and transportation in Co. Donegal, 1836–42' in Bob Reece (ed.), *Irish convicts: the origins of convicts transported to Australia* (Dublin, 1989), pp 129–9; Brenda Mooney, 'Women convicts from Wexford and Waterford, 1836–1840' in Reece (ed.), *Irish convicts*, pp 115–27; Leonora Irwin, 'Women convicts from Dublin,

Primary sources for the study of crime

The petitions usually contain some explanation by the prisoners or their relatives as to why clemency should be exercised. These statements of mitigating circumstances should not be taken at face value, of course, as they are clearly self-serving documents. Nevertheless, they offer what is frequently a valuable alternative explanation of the offenders' actions from those advanced by policemen, magistrates or others engaged in the enforcement of law and order which the researcher can take into account along with other evidence. The petitions often contain letters of support from clergymen, justices of the peace and other people of standing in the community. All petitions for clemency were investigated. The lord lieutenant referred them, via the Chief Secretary's Office, to the trial judge, the local constabulary, and sometimes to the governor of the appropriate gaol to confirm statements made by the prisoners regarding their innocence or mitigating circumstances, such as their extreme poverty or their having large families. These investigations often generated quite bulky files detailing such matters as the prisoners' criminal records and information on their family backgrounds, which should serve as an invaluable source for the researcher. The accumulated documents that resulted from the investigations into prisoners' petitions are known as Prisoners' Petitions and Cases from 1778 to 1835, and Convict Reference Files from 1836 to 1922.[38] There are more than 10,000 convict petitions available from 1836 onwards.[39] A similar series of petitions from offenders found guilty of less serious offences and sentenced to less than one year in prison or to a monetary fine, the Criminal Index Files, exists for the period from 1842 to 1920. The finding aid for the Prisoners' Petitions and Cases is a card index in the reading room, while the finding aids for the Convict Reference Files and the Criminal Index Files are some fifteen Convict Reference Books and seventeen Criminal Index Books, respectively. These give brief, and sometimes sparse, summaries of the individual cases: for instance, it was not until 1860 that the Convict Reference Books began to record the crimes committed by the petitioners. The finding aids should provide enough detail for the researcher seeking to find information on individual criminals or prisoners and their crimes or misdemeanours; they are more difficult tools for the researcher interested in exploring the general history of crime, but when used with care and diligence they should enable one to unearth valuable supplementary detail about individual crimes or types of crime at local level.

The following examples indicate the type of evidence that awaits the historian who probes behind the rather sparse detail contained in the finding aids. Take the case of Alexander Mullin in 1853, for instance. The Convict Reference Book

1836–40' in Reece (ed.), *Irish convicts*, pp 161–91; Sinead Curley, 'Transportation in Clare before and after the Famine' in Reece (ed.), *Irish convicts*, pp 81–113; Elizabeth Steiner-Scott, '"To bounce a boot off her now & then ...": domestic violence in post-Famine Ireland' in Maryann Gialanella Valiulis and Mary O'Dowd (eds), *Women and Irish history: essays in honour of Margaret MacCurtain* (Dublin, 1997), pp 125–43; Frank Sweeney, *The murder of Conell Boyle, County Donegal, 1898* (Dublin, 2002). **38** Rena Lohan, 'Sources in the National Archives for research into the transportation of Irish convicts to Australia (1791–1853)' in *Irish Archives* (spring 1996), p. 25. **39** Cosgrave, Lohan and Quinlan, 'Sources for researching the Great Famine', p. 37.

To The Right Honorable
Robert Offley Ashburton
Baron Houghton
Lord Lieutenant General and General
Governor of Ireland

The Humble Petition of Adam Brockie of 31 Aberdeen Street in the City of Dublin

May it please Your Excellency

That on the 7th day of January my son aged eight years was waiting to enter a school entertainment and took up a handfull of snow not with the intention of throwing it at any passenger, but to throw at a Companion when he was arrested and fined ten shillings by the Magistrate

That at the time of the arrest I was lying sick in bed

That after my recovery my wife took ill and has since died

That I have been at great expense owing to the illness and death of my wife and my own sickness

Under the foregoing Circumstances May it please Your Excellency to exempt me from the fine imposed by the Magistrate

And your petitioner will ever pray

3 Extract from Adam Brockie's appeal to the lord lieutenant for clemency for his son, Criminal Index Files, CIF 1895/ B18 (courtesy of the National Archives, Ireland).

for that year merely records his name, the fact that his unspecified crime was committed in Tyrone, that he was sentenced to death, that his appeal to the lord lieutenant for clemency met with an unfavourable response, and that he was executed. On ordering the documents relating to Mullin's case, using the details provided in the Convict Reference Book, one finds out a lot more about the circumstances that brought Mullin to the hangman's noose. The 24-year-old had been living with his parents at Ballyweaney, Loughguile, County Antrim before going to reside with his aunt at Kirkpatrick, County Tyrone. According to Judge Torrens, who tried Mullin's case at Tyrone assizes in Omagh in July 1853, he murdered his 70-year-old aunt after she had paid him his wages and told him that she 'did not wish him further to remain with her, as he did little work & she was unable to support him'. The jury in the case pleaded for mercy as they regarded Mullin's act 'as that of a man who, from extreme ignorance and apparent deficiency of intellect, seemed incapable of comprehending his position with want to moral responsibility'. They believed his deed was not premeditated, and that he had been convicted on circumstantial evidence. The memorial of various inhabitants of Omagh, among them three Protestant clergymen, three Catholic priests and six justices of the peace, pleaded for mercy on a number of grounds, including the fact that 'the judge when passing sentence dwelt strongly on the prisoner's ignorance of the first principles of our common religion; and that he heard with astonishment that the prisoner at the time of his committal for murder did not know the name of the Saviour'. The Presbyterian prison chaplain, who paid frequent visits to Mullin while he was incarcerated, confirmed the prisoner's ignorance of 'even the plainest views of the system of salvation'.[40] The files of John McCarthy's case in 1870 further show how worthwhile it is to delve deeper into the details supplied in the finding aid. The Convict Reference Book merely records McCarthy's name, the fact that he was convicted of 'Whiteboyism' at the Limerick special commission on 19 June 1867, and that his appeal met with an unfavourable response from the lord lieutenant. On ordering McCarthy's case documents from the Convict Reference Files, one discovers that he was not a 'Whiteboy' at all but was, instead, a principal in the Fenian attack on Kilmallock barracks during the 1867 rising. He was one of the armed guard over the two quarrymen who were forced to drill a hole in the barracks wall in an attempt to blow up the building. McCarthy's offence was incorrectly recorded as a 'Whiteboy' offence because he was arrested under the so-called Whiteboy Act for having arms in a proclaimed district, a charge to which he pleaded guilty, according to Resident Magistrate D.B. Franks of Bruff, in order to escape more serious charges connected with his involvement in the rebellion. Further police and informer evidence builds up a damning case against the car-man's son, who, apparently, neither initiated the plea for clemency nor signed it, and it is unsurprising that the lord lieutenant ordered 'Let the law take its course' in this case.[41] Finally, there is the case of Robert Brockie in 1895. The Criminal Index Book for 1895 tells us his

---

40 Convict Reference Files, CRF 1853/M32.   **41** Ibid., CRF 1867/Mc31.

name, that the location of his offence was Dublin city, that his offence was 'Snowballing', and that he was fined ten shillings for this misdemeanour. Young Brockie's case was the subject of a petition from his father (see illustration 3), and an enquiry from the under-secretary of Ireland into the details of the case! The under-secretary's correspondence with officials at the DMP court at Inn's Quay, where the boy's case was tried, led to his writing to the lord lieutenant to state that

> No doubt [Police Magistrate] Mr O'Donel felt it necessary to prevent inconvenience to the public, while a supply of snow so tempting to boys lay on the ground: but as the snow has now disappeared I think His Excellency might be graciously pleased to remit the penalty on this young delinquent, who does not appear to have hurt any one or to have meant to do so.

In this case, the lord lieutenant exercised his prerogative of mercy and remitted the boy's fine.[42] As these three cases demonstrate, the prisoners' petitions are an important source for the historian of crime, providing evocative details that are often absent from other contemporary sources.

Another potentially useful source are the Penal Record Files, containing details of convicts who were released on licence from 1882 to 1895. These are part of the General Prisons Board Papers, the huge administrative section that oversaw the running of prisons in Ireland. The Penal Record Files contain mundane details of convicts' illnesses, punishments, visitors and the names of persons with whom convicts were in correspondence while serving their sentences: such information is not of particular interest to the historian of crime. What is worth noting, however, is that the Penal Record Files contain two photographs of each convict – one taken on reception into prison, and one taken on release from incarceration. Such rare photographic evidence has been used to good effect by Geraldine Curtin, *The women of Galway jail: female criminality in nineteenth-century Ireland* (Galway and Dublin, 2001).[43]

(e) Documents for the study of Fenianism: police and crime records

The National Archives is the most important repository for researchers wishing to investigate the local history of Fenianism.[44] As with the State of the Country Papers, Outrage Papers and Chief Secretary's Office Registered Papers, much of this material consists of reports sent by police and magistrates to Dublin Castle on the activities of local sus-

---

42 Criminal Index Files, CIF 1895/B18.   **43** The Penal Record Files also provide brief details of each prisoner's crime, residence of family or next of kin, marital status, place of abode, religion, occupation and physical description.   **44** Breandán Mac Giolla Choille, 'Fenian documents in the State Paper Office' in *Irish Historical Studies*, xvi, no. 63 (1969), pp 258–84 is a useful introduction to this material. Researchers should note that the State Paper Office is no longer in existence, and its records have been transferred to the National Archives.

pects. Some of the most valuable reports were supplied to the police or magistrates by informers from within the organisation. A portion of the Fenian material also consists of documents seized in the police raid on the *Irish People* offices in September 1865, as well as other papers found on Fenian suspects from 1858 onwards. Overall, the National Archives of Ireland material relating to the Fenian movement allows the researcher to gain a fascinating insight into the mundane, day-to-day activities of the rank and file members of the organisation, as well as the activities of the leadership.

Most of the Fenian material forms part of the Police and Crime Records, a subsection (consisting of 40 cartons and 12 bound volumes) of the Chief Secretary's Office Papers. There is a bound finding aid to this material at the issue desk of the reading room.[45] The earliest Police and Crime Records documents are the Police Reports on Secret Societies, dating from September 1857 to July 1859. Most of these papers, which are uncatalogued, are from 1858. The activities of the Phoenix Society in Cork and Kerry form a major subject of these papers,[46] and there is also a sizeable file on the early Fenian movement in Kilkenny (although the police and magistrates do not use this term, it is clear to the historian that this is what they are, in fact, describing). There is also a small amount of material on early Fenian (and some Ribbon) activity in Antrim, Cavan, Fermanagh, Kilkenny, Leitrim, Mayo, Meath, Sligo, Tipperary and Wicklow. Many of the documents are police accounts of Catholic priests' sermons denouncing the presence of treasonable secret societies in their parishes.

The Reports on Fenianism 1864–65 are a larger collection of papers. Most of these reports come from resident magistrates, members of the Irish Constabulary and Detective Superintendent Daniel Ryan of the DMP, who received valuable regular reports from Pierce Nagle, a disgruntled Fenian with regular access to the offices of the *Irish People*, one of the nerve centres of the Fenian organisation, not just for Dublin members but for those from all parts of Ireland. This collection also contains some reports from the Home Office, Foreign Office and the London Metropolitan Police, but most of the material relates to the activities of the Fenians in Ireland.[47]

The Fenian Papers, which document the years from 1866 to 1874, are the most substantial single part of the Police and Crime Records relating to Fenianism. The Fenian Papers or F Papers commence in February 1866 and are probably those which Samuel Lee Anderson, assistant to the Irish attorney-general, James A. Lawson, selected from the correspondence to the Chief Secretary's Office dealing with the Fenian organisation. The selection appears to have been made, in the initial stages, to discover those documents which would assist the staff involved in dealing with the issuing of warrants under the Habeas Corpus Suspension Act in 1866. In the course of time, however, the basis of selection was enlarged and for the years 1866–1867 the F Papers and Registered Papers of the Chief Secretary's Office[48] are

---

[45] 'P&C Fenian Papers 1858/1883'. [46] Seán Ó Lúing, 'The Phoenix Society in Kerry, 1858–9' in *Kerry Archaeological and Historical Society Journal*, no. 2 (1969), pp 5–26 makes good use of these files. [47] A bound volume, 'Fenianism, index of names 1864–65' gives the source, date and subject of the reports on Fenian suspects. [48] The amount of correspondence relating to Fenianism in the Registered Papers is enormous. There is a bound, typescript calendar of this material available at the National Archives

the main sources in the National Archives for the study of Fenianism. From 1866 to 1874 they are the single most important source dealing with Fenianism.[49] In the latter period, the F Papers deal principally with such matters as the arrest, prosecution and discharge of persons in custody on suspicion or on charges of Fenianism; 'Manchester Martyr' processions in Ireland; amnesty movement meetings; the illegal importation of arms and ammunition, or robbery to acquire them; illegal drilling; crown witnesses and offers of information; the assassination of suspected informers; rumours of planned rebellions; the movements of prominent Fenians and meetings held by them, and the activities of less prominent members and suspected members of the organisation.[50]

Another useful source is the collection known as the Fenian Briefs. These are mainly printed briefs in the case of the leading Fenian suspects who were tried in the 1860s, along with witness statements and the material seized in the raids on the *Irish People* offices and other incriminating evidence. As well as throwing light on the illicit activities of the Fenians in the mid-1860s, the Crown Briefs are also useful for a behind-the-scenes view of the business operations of the *Irish People* newspaper, including its local agents nation-wide.

Researchers will also find the bound volume 'Fenianism, index of names, 1866–71' of considerable interest. This includes the names, addresses, occupations and brief details of arrested Fenians and of Fenian suspects, including those arrested under the Habeas Corpus Suspension Act. The criteria for featuring suspects' names in this index are not entirely clear. Many rank and file members' details appear to have been included as well as those of leaders at local level, for instance, and many of the names of priests who took part in 'Manchester Martyr' or Amnesty Association meetings[51] are also documented: a loose definition of what constituted Fenian activity seems to have been used when compiling this list of names. This source may still be used with advantage by the historian of Fenianism at the local level, provided it is consulted with care. It is particularly informative in that it indicates the rank of individual 'A's, 'B's, 'C's and 'D's in various localities, when these were known, or suspected, by the local constabulary. The index is often the only surviving source for this information.

enquiry desk. **49** Mac Giolla Choille, 'Fenian documents', p. 277. The papers from February 1866 to December 1867, numbers 105 to 5076, are numbered in black ink with the letter 'F' prefixed; those from January 1868 to December 1874, numbers 5 to 9135, are numbered in red ink with a red letter 'R' suffixed. Following contemporary practice in the Chief Secretary's Office, one uses these prefixes and suffixes when ordering and referring to these papers: for example, Fenian Papers F1177 or 9134R. **50** Ibid., p.278. For examples of secondary sources that have drawn on the Fenian Papers to study the Fenian movement at the local level see R.V. Comerford, 'Patriotism as pastime: the appeal of Fenianism in the mid-1860s' in *Irish Historical Studies*, xxii, no. 87 (1981), pp 239–50; Brian Griffin, 'Social aspects of Fenianism in Leinster and Connacht, 1858–1870' in *Éire-Ireland*, xxi, no. 1 (spring 1986), pp 16–39. **51** It was perfectly possible to oppose the Fenian movement, but still feel sympathy for the men executed at Manchester and the Fenian prisoners who were incarcerated for some years after the failure of the 1867 rebellion. See the discussion in R.V. Comerford, *The Fenians in context: Irish politics and society, 1848–82* (Dublin, 1998 edition), pp 148–9 and Gerard Moran, *A radical priest in Mayo: Fr Patrick Lavelle: the rise and fall of an Irish nationalist, 1825–86* (Dublin, 1994), pp 100–1.

The last source of note within the Police and Crime Records for the study of Fenianism in Ireland[52] is the Fenian Photograph collection. This consists of photographs and descriptions of prisoners detained under the Habeas Corpus Suspension Act from 1866 to 1868 and Fenian suspects in later years, including a number of 'Ribbon' suspects in the early 1870s.[53] There are approximately 600 documents in this collection – about half of them comprising of both photographs and descriptions, while the remainder give descriptions of the suspects only. The descriptions feature details of each suspect's name, age, literacy level, religion, marital status, occupation, place of birth and residence, place of residence of his parents, and a physical description of the suspect. As these are not convicts, the photographs show the suspects in civilian clothes, with full heads of hair, beards and moustaches (except, of course, when the prisoners were bald or balding and did not grow facial hair!). There is a card index to this material in the reading room of the National Archives.

The researcher should also be aware that the Police and Crime Records contain two sources that have no direct bearing on the history of the Fenian movement in this period. The first is a bound collection of some 116 threatening letters of an agrarian nature, mostly posted in Westmeath in 1868 and 1869, although there is also a small number posted in King's County, Meath, Mayo and Kildare. A letter dated November 1869 and sent to Thomas Moran of Streamstown, County Westmeath, provides a good flavour of the contents of this material:

> Thomas Moran, I hereby command you to give up the Lands you hold in Streamstown that is Cline's and Kenny's. Now I order you under pain of instant death to give it up to the man who is the true owner of it a man that you deprived of it by injustice and deceit treachery and robbery. I am going round through this country recalling all lands lost by injustice and if you don't give back the said lands I will meet you with a clean rifle, dry powder, an Irish heart, a correct eye and steady finger. You must give it up to the man you deprived of it or I will burn a bullet hole through you as you burnt the house formerly to deprive him of it.
> God Save Ireland
> Erin-go-Braugh   Rory of the Hill[54]

---

52 This source contains another collection of material, the A Files, for the years 1864–8 and 1877–83. This consists of consular despatches from the United States, and Home Office reports on the IRB. Most of this material relates to Fenianism in either the United States or Britain. While there is some Irish material, it is only a fraction of the overall collection.   **53** For two examples see W.E. Vaughan (ed.), *A new history of Ireland, v. Ireland under the Union, I 1801–70* (Oxford, 1989), illustrations 38b and 38c. There is also a smaller sample of suspects' photographs in a bound volume, 'Description of Fenian suspects 1866–1872', that the researcher may also wish to consult. Most of the photographs and descriptive details of the forty-five individuals recorded in this volume are of so-called 'Ribbonmen', or men suspected of involvement in agrarian outrages, particularly in Westmeath and Meath. This volume, ICR 16, is part of the Irish Crimes Records collection, which is discussed in a separate section of this guide at pp 41–3.   **54** Police and Crime Records, threatening letters. As the originals are fading and fragile, the researcher is given a bound collection of photographic facsimiles of the original documents

This is an important source, as the threatening letter (when genuine) constitutes one of the few types of primary evidence for understanding or interpreting crime that does not originate from a policeman, magistrate or other functionary.

The second source are the so-called Irish National League Papers 1879 to 1889 which, as the dates indicate, also include some material relating to the Land League.[55] This collection consists of ten cartons of documents, mostly comprising police reports of speeches by members of the National League and proceedings of the organisation at the local level, reports of intimidation practised by National League branches (mainly in counties Clare and Kerry), copies of documents submitted to the *Times* special commission on 'Parnellism' and crime, and some seized National League correspondence and papers.[56]

(f) Papers of the Chief Crown Solicitor, and Crown Files at assizes and quarter sessions

The National Archives of Ireland also holds documents produced by the machinery of justice that the historian of crime will find useful. In 1801 six crown solicitors, one for each assizes circuit, were appointed to act as prosecutors at assizes.[57] Beginning in 1846, crown solicitors were distributed over counties instead of being confined to the circuits: there were some twenty of these officials by 1880. In addition to the crown solicitors there was a crown and treasury solicitor who acted as the government's chief crown solicitor. The business of prosecuting cases at assizes was entrusted to these officials, while the chief crown solicitor offered legal advice to the government. From 1820 the government appointed sessional crown solicitors whose task was to prosecute for the crown at quarter sessions.[58] These officials produced much paperwork that provides another useful source for the researcher.

The Chief Crown Solicitor's Papers from 1859 to 1890 largely consist of requests for advice from police and magistrates about how to proceed in specific cases, and the replies of the chief crown solicitor to these requests. The correspondence concerning individual cases is often substantial, although some cases were dealt with very briefly. The subject matter varies widely. A number of cases were almost certainly unique affairs from which the historian of crime can learn little of a general nature. For instance, one file addresses a query in 1865 over whether justices at quarter sessions had the power to imprison a drunk train driver for two years, with or without hard labour, if he was employed as a driver by one railway company, and

---

to consult. **55** These papers are catalogued in a finding aid at the enquiry desk, 'P & C Police Reports 1848/1921'. **56** The National League is discussed in Laurence M. Geary, *The plan of campaign, 1886–1891* (Cork, 1986) and Donald M. Jordan, 'The Irish National League and the "unwritten law": rural protest and nation-building in Ireland 1882–1892' in *Past & Present*, no. 158 (Feb. 1998), pp 146–71. **57** For a discussion of the operation of the assizes in one county see Desmond McCabe, '"That part that laws or kings can cause or cure": crown prosecutions and jury trial at Longford assizes, 1830–45' in Raymond Gillespie and Gerard Moran (eds), *Longford: essays in county history* (Dublin, 1991), pp 153–72. **58** John F. McEldowney, 'Crown prosecutions in nineteenth-century Ireland' in Douglas Hay and Francis Snyder (eds), *Policing and prosecution in Britain, 1750–1850* (Oxford, 1989), pp 435, 443; McDowell, *Irish administration*, pp 121–2.

a servant by another, and was driving a train while technically employed as a servant.[59] Others are of more general interest, such as the file dealing with the query in 1869 from the justices of the peace of Dublin City about whether velocipedes should be considered as vehicles and their riders subject to the same penalties as persons who rode or drove 'furiously' on any thoroughfare: this case arose after the magistrates complained that they had 'received many complaints regarding the very dangerous practice of persons riding on velocipedes on the Public Footways'.[60] The usefulness of the Chief Crown Solicitor's Papers to the researcher, then, will depend on the type of crime or offence that one is interested in researching. The results of consulting this material can be very rewarding. Take, as a final example, the substantial file regarding the case of a threatening notice posted at the home of a King's County police pensioner and farmer, and a threatening letter sent to the same address, in February 1860. The notice, posted by 'a true friend of Mollymaguire', warned Benjamin Roe of Ballycue to give up his farm or he would be 'shot as dead as a magit'. The letter, from 'Molly's true son', stated that Roe had forfeited his life as he had failed to give up his farm as advised in the notice, and that he and his family would be shot. An investigation by Head Constable Carolin concluded that the person responsible for the threatening notice and letter was Roe's daughter – a search warrant led to the discovery in her copybook of several sketches of coffins similar to the coffin on the threatening notice, and the edges of torn pages in the copybook matched exactly the edges of the threatening notice and letter. Her object was, it was believed, that she shought to have a protection party stationed in her father's house. She was, apparently, in love with Sub-Constable Andrew Purcell of the Geashill station, to whom she had written poems: reading between the lines, it seems she hoped that Purcell would be one of the protection party! Resident Magistrate Warburton of Tullamore was determined to prosecute her, writing on 24 April 1860 that

> I certainly look on this case as one of great importance as it will shew the people that when fabricated crime is detected the authorities are as anxious to expose and punish it as any other and from my experience I fear many of the threatening notices &c are such but it is almost impossible to detect them.[61]

This evidence suggests that the researcher should be careful not to take all threatening notices and letters at face value, a topic returned to in the pages below.[62]

The researcher will also find much useful material in the Crown Files at assizes and quarter sessions.[63] These consist of prosecutors' briefs, which contain the evidence used to build a case against the accused in jury trials.[64] This evidence includes

59 Chief Crown Solicitor's Papers, CCS 1865/373.   **60** Ibid., CCS 1869/158.   **61** Ibid., CCS 1860/90.   **62** See p. 66.   **63** For a discussion of this source see Carolyn A. Conley, 'Irish criminal records, 1865–1892' in *Éire-Ireland*, xxviii (1993), pp 97–106.   **64** For a discussion of the Irish system of trial by jury see John F. McEldowney, 'Policing and the administration of justice in nineteenth-century Ireland'

scene-of-crime reports, witness depositions, and accounts of the progress of police and magistrate investigations into solving particular crimes, as well as related correspondence between Dublin Castle and crown and sessional solicitors. Many Chief Secretary's Office Registered Papers are thus to be found in these Crown Briefs. The Crown Files at assizes and quarter sessions are a potentially invaluable source for the historian researching serious crimes, as they often enable one to piece together a detailed picture of the background to individual crimes,[65] as well as providing a foundation for a more wide-ranging examination of specific types of crime, particularly crimes of violence. Carolyn Conley has made excellent use of Crown Files in her study of 'violence as recreation' in post-Famine Ireland[66] and violence against women,[67] as well as the general phenomenon of violence in post-Famine Irish society.[68] One should bear in mind, however, that the Crown Files, although of immense value, are patchy and often in a very fragile condition. They used to be stored in the Public Record Office and most were lost in the destruction of the Four Courts archive in 1922. No Crown Files survive for certain counties, while there are only fragmentary files for others. Furthermore, what remains often bears tell-tale signs of the fire at the Four Courts, hence one may need the special permission of one the National Archives archivists to use this material. Some Crown Files are available in the Public Record Office of Northern Ireland.[69] The National Archives has an incomplete collection of the correspondence and note-books of the Tipperary crown solicitor for 1901–1903 and 1909–1920,[70] while the National Library holds some of the papers, including Crown Briefs, of Thomas L. Cooke, sessional solicitor for King's County and Samuel Lee Anderson, crown solicitor for Kilkenny, from 1839 to 1848 and from 1876 to 1877, respectively.[71]

The National Archives of Ireland also holds the order book of Collon petty sessions from July 1828 to July 1833,[72] which should enable the Louth historian to build up a picture of the incidence of minor offences and the litigious nature of the local community in this period. The National Library of Ireland has similar petty sessions material for Westport, County Mayo from 1823 to 1824, Stranorlar, County

---

in Clive Emsley and Barbara Weinberger (eds), *Policing Western Europe: politics, professionalism, and public order, 1850–1940* (New York, Westport, Ct., and London, 1991), pp 18–35; David Johnson, 'Trial by jury in Ireland 1860–1914' in *Legal History*, 17, no. 3 (Dec. 1996), pp 270–93. **65** The Crown files at the 1865 Meath assizes were invaluable in making sense of the issues involved in the December 1864 murder of a landlord's agent in Rathcore, County Meath. See Brian Griffin, 'An agrarian murder and evictions in Rathcore' in *Ríocht na Midhe*, ix, no. 1 (1994–5), pp 88–103. **66** Carolyn A. Conley, 'The agreeable recreation of fighting' in *Journal of Social History*, 33, no. 1 (autumn 1999), pp 57–67. For a brief discussion of what was, at least in part, recreational fighting in post-Famine Tipperary see Christy O'Dwyer, 'Archbishop Leahy and faction fighting' in *Tipperary Historical Journal* (1989), pp 20–26. **67** Carolyn A. Conley, 'No pedestals: women and violence in late nineteenth-century Ireland' in *Journal of Social History*, 28 (summer 1995), pp 801–18. **68** Carolyn A. Conley, *Melancholy accidents: the meaning of violence in post-Famine Ireland* (Lanham, 1999); idem, 'Homicide in late-Victorian Ireland and Scotland' in *New Hibernia Review*, 5, no. 3 (autumn 2001), pp 66–86. **69** Public Record Office of Northern Ireland, 66 Balmoral Avenue, Belfast BT9 6NY. **70** Co. 1973–1974 (correspondence and assize briefs), M3049 (solicitor's notebooks). **71** MS. 25298, MSS 11265–11267. **72** M4919.

Donegal from 1851 to 1921 (with most of the material dating from 1851 to 1873), Loughrea, County Galway from 1866 to 1869 and 1895 to 1904, Clonbur, County Galway from 1880 to 1897 and Ballybay, County Monaghan from 1895 to 1900.[73]

(g) Irish Crimes Records

The Irish Crimes Records are part of the Chief Secretary's Office Papers. They consist of bound volumes that vary in their content and subject matter. The most useful material are the abstracts of the cases of prisoners who were arrested under the provisions of the Habeas Corpus Suspension Act from 1866 to 1868,[74] the printed returns of outrages reported to the Constabulary Office in Dublin Castle from 1844 to 1893,[75] and the five-volume register of abstracts of the cases of some 987 suspects arrested under the Protection of Person and Property (Ireland) Act of 1881.[76]

The three-volume 'Habeas Corpus Suspension Act, Abstracts of Cases', with an additional index volume, consists of abstracts of the cases against some 1,476 suspects arrested from 1866 to 1868 on suspicion of involvement in the Fenian movement, including the 1867 rebellion. Such features as details of the suspects' names, ages, occupations and their alleged Fenian activities, or the grounds for suspicion against them, are invaluable for the historian trying to piece together details of the organisation at local level. These volumes are particularly important as many of the abstracts come from various Chief Secretary's Office documents which have been subsequently lost – they thus constitute, in many cases, the only surviving evidence of why the constabulary or magistrates wished to have these individuals arrested. One should read these abstracts with some caution, as it is clear from a close perusal of their details that certain suspects were arrested who had absolutely no connection with Fenianism, a fact which should have been apparent to the constabulary at the time. For example, Lawrence Maher, a publican from Michael Street, Waterford, was arrested in March 1866, apparently on the basis of a report from the local sub-inspector of constabulary that he 'keeps a house noted for Fenian meetings and the resort of soldiers many of whom he has no doubt took the Fenian oath in his house'. After his arrest, Maher submitted a memorial in which he denied ever having taken any part in the Fenian conspiracy, 'but on the contrary was most particular in refusing drink to any suspected parties and frequently turned parties out of his house for singing Fenian songs'. This version of events was supported in an affidavit by an eyewitness, but the authorities still decided on 3 May 1866 to detain Maher in custody. Several other memorials followed from Maher and other inhabitants of Waterford, including a member of parliament, before he was eventually discharged on bail on 17 September 1866.[77] Another arrested suspect who was clearly

---

[73] Westport petty sessions book, MS. 14902; Stranorlar petty sessions minute book, microfilm n.3913 p.3584; Loughrea petty sessions book, MSS 93–93a; papers of Ballybay town court, MS. 13782; Clonbur sub-district crime and offence register, MS. 2193. [74] Irish Crimes Records, ICR 10–13. [75] Irish Crimes Records, ICR 1–4. These returns do not include details of crimes committed in the DMP district. [76] These abstracts of cases are analysed in Clark, 'Social composition'. [77] Details from Habeas Corpus Suspension Act, abstracts of cases, ii, p. 135.

innocent was a Glenamaddy labourer, James McPheely. According to the constable at Glenamaddy, he was arrested 'under very suspicious circumstances' on 9 March 1867. The constable explained that McPheely had declared himself 'the Head Centre for Europe', as well as James Stephens! Eventually McPheely was lodged in Mountjoy prison. There, he was examined by the gaol's medical officer, who certified on 7 June that he 'appears to be a monomaniac' and unfit for imprisonment. McPheely's discharge was ordered on 15 June 1867.[78] Although there are probably details of other cases of innocent prisoners in these volumes, there is also no doubt that most of the prisoners whose activities are described in them were leading members of the IRB throughout Ireland. A careful reading of the abstracts allows one to build up quite a good picture, from the perspective of the forces of law and order, of the personnel and activities of the Fenian movement at local level.[79]

When using the Irish Crimes Records Returns of Outrages, one should note that the earlier returns are in statistical form and would be difficult for the local historian to use, as the county is the smallest geographical unit featured in these returns. From 1857 onwards an important additional category – brief particulars of each homicide committed – was incorporated into the returns. These particulars give details of the date of each homicide, the circumstances as far as they were known to the constabulary, the names of suspects, and brief details of the progress of the investigation and the results of the trial (if any were held) of the suspects. In the returns of 1869 the RIC began recording particulars of all cases of firing at the person in a similar manner to their detailing of homicides, which also included ascribing motives to these crimes; from 1871, similar details were given in all instances of firing into dwelling houses. Such synopses of the more serious crimes help the researcher in trying to interpret what the outrage statistics tell us about crime in post-Famine Ireland.[80]

The Registers of Arrests of Suspects under the Protection of Person and Property Act are an essential source for the study of the Land War in the early 1880s.[81] The Abstracts of Prisoners' Cases provide useful biographical details and accounts of the actions of some of the leading Land League activists at the local level, as well as of men suspected of involvement in agrarian outrages. The abstracts give details of each suspect's name, place of residence, occupation, and a précis of the crime for which the suspect was arrested or a précis of the other grounds on which he was suspected by the police. One should be aware that the individuals noted in the registers are suspects only, and were not found guilty of any crime. Indeed, in many, and perhaps most, cases in the registers it is apparent that the RIC were using the powers granted to them under the Protection of Person and Property Act to detain without trial persons against whom they could not otherwise obtain satisfactory evidence that would hold up in a court of law.[82] A case in point is that of Michael

---

78 Details from ibid., unnumbered page between pp 292 and 293.   **79** The abstracts have been used by R.V. Comerford to map the strength of Fenianism in each Irish county in the 1866–8 period. See his *Fenians in context*, p. 117.   **80** The outrage returns are analysed in Vaughan, *Landlords and tenants in mid-Victorian Ireland*, passim.   **81** Irish Crimes Records, ICR 5–9.   **82** For the opinion of contemporary officials that this was, indeed, the constabulary's general approach to their duty during the Land

Ryan of Nenagh, County Tipperary. On the night of 27 May 1881 the houses of Michael Mackey, Michael Broder and John Nolan were visited by several men who threatened the three householders. Ryan was duly arrested, the 'evidence' against him being that he was secretary of the Nenagh branch of the Land League, that he was a stationer (John Nolan said that the men who threatened him 'appeared well dressed & very like shop boys'), that he had been seen by Sub-inspector Reeves 'endeavouring to obstruct a bailiff', and that he was reputed to be one of the principals behind the system of intimidation in the area.[83] John Sweeny, a publican and carpenter from Loughrea, County Galway, was arrested on suspicion of being an accessory to the murders of James Connors and Patrick Dempsey on 1 May 1881 and 29 May 1881, respectively. The police gave their grounds for suspicion against Sweeny as follows: 'A prominent L. Leaguer. Secret meetings held in his house. He employed an attorney to defend the prisoners charged with the murders of Connors & Dempsey and supplied them with food'.[84] The evidence against both Ryan and Sweeny was circumstantial at best, and the same can be said about a sizeable proportion of the other suspects, at least to judge by the details given in the register. There was more damning evidence against other suspects, however. For instance, Thomas B. Kelly, a farmer of Rockhill, Aranmore, County Galway, was arrested on suspicion of being involved in swearing in members of an unnamed secret society. Suspicion fell on Kelly after he took out of his pocket a piece of paper containing a form of illegal oath and handed it in mistake for another paper to the assistant petty sessions clerk at Galway on 24 December 1880.[85] Another suspect, James Higgins of Clonmellon, County Westmeath, who worked as an assistant to his father, a publican and farmer, was arrested after two threatening notices were posted to John Murphy of Moygrehan on 30 December 1880 and 4 January 1881, warning him to give up his farm, in consequence of which he surrendered his holding. One of the notices was signed by Higgins![86]

The final volume of material that is particularly important in the Irish Crimes Records is entitled 'Intelligence notes: prosecutions, 1887–91'.[87] This consists of printed accounts of court cases, most of which were high-profile prosecutions of newspaper editors, members of parliament, clergymen and other leaders of the land agitation under the Criminal Law and Procedure Act of 1887. The volume includes police reports and extracts from contemporary newspapers of seditious speeches by leaders of the land agitation or newspaper accounts detailing the activities of suppressed branches of the National League, as well as accounts of boycotting, resistance to evictions and various forms of intimidation that constituted part of the tactics used in the Land War in the later 1880s and early 1890s.[88]

War see Charles Dalton Clifford Lloyd, *Ireland under the Land League: a narrative of personal experiences* (Edinburgh and London, 1892), p. 226; Sir Henry Robinson, *Memories: wise and otherwise* (London, 1924), pp 31–33.   **83** ICR 5, i, no. 129.   **84** Ibid., no. 145.   **85** Ibid., no. 4.   **86** Ibid., no. 35.   **87** ICR 22.   **88** For an account of the application of the Criminal Law and Procedure (Ireland) Act against a single individual see Laurence M. Geary, 'John Mandeville and the Irish Crimes Act of 1887' in *Irish Historical Studies*, xxv, no. 100 (Nov. 1987), pp 358–75.

(h) Crime Special Branch Reports

The Land War of the late 1870s and early 1880s caused severe strain on the RIC and led to important changes in the force's procedures in preventing and detecting agrarian and political offences and monitoring the individuals and organisations responsible for these offences.[89] Some changes, such as the greatly increased use of the military in aid of the civil power, were temporary expedients.[90] A more important and permanent development was the creation on 1 October 1883 of the Crime Special Branch of the RIC, to monitor and combat the activities of agrarian and political secret societies. This was a refinement of an earlier shake up of the RIC's approach to agrarian and political crime in August 1882, when the post of Under-Secretary for Police and Crime was instituted to streamline police crime-fighting and intelligence-gathering methods. This post was held by Edward G. Jenkinson.[91] Under Jenkinson, in December 1881 six Special Resident Magistrates were appointed to oversee police and military activity in fifteen counties or parts of counties.[92] On 1 July 1882 the scheme was expanded to cover some twenty counties.[93] The office of Special Resident Magistrate ceased on 30 September 1883, and on 1 October 1883 the Special Resident Magistrates were replaced by four officers who were designated Divisional Magistrates (later re-named Divisional Commissioners in 1889). These were in charge of overseeing police activity against secret societies in four new divisions: the Midland, Western, South-western and South-eastern;[94] a Northern Division, dealing with secret society activities in most of Ulster and in Louth, was created in October 1885.[95] The Divisional Commissioners were even-

89 See R.A.J. Hawkins, 'Government versus secret societies: the Parnell era' in Williams (ed.), *Secret societies*, pp 100–12. **90** David N. Haire, 'In aid of the civil power, 1868–90' in Lyons and Hawkins (eds), *Ireland under the Union*, pp 115–47; R.A.J. Hawkins, 'An army on police work, 1881–2: Ross of Bladensburg's memorandum' in the *Irish Sword*, xi (1973), pp 75–117. **91** Details from Stephen Ball (ed.), *A policeman's Ireland: recollections of Samuel Waters, RIC* (Cork, 1999), pp 12–13, 100; Leon Ó Broin, *The prime informer: a suppressed scandal* (London, 1971), pp 21–2; Breandán Mac Giolla Choille (ed.), *Intelligence notes, 1913–16* (Dublin, 1966), p. xxiii. For a discussion of the Special Branch in the early twentieth century see W.F. Mandle, 'Sir Anthony MacDonnell and Crime Branch Special' in MacDonagh and Mandle (eds), *Ireland and Irish-Australia*, pp 175–94. **92** The Special Resident Magistrates, and their respective areas of responsibility were Captain Owen Slacke (Waterford, Tipperary and Cork (East Riding)), Henry A. Blake (Galway (East Riding), King's County, and Queen's County), T.O. Plunkett (Kerry and Cork (West Riding)), Captain A.S. Butler (Westmeath, Longford and Leitrim), Charles Dalton Clifford Lloyd (Limerick and Clare) and Colonel W. Forbes (Mayo, Sligo and Roscommon). **93** The officers and the extent of their respective areas of responsibility under the revised scheme were Colonel W. Forbes (Sligo, Mayo, Roscommon), Clifford Lloyd (Galway, Clare and Limerick), T.O. Plunkett (Cork and Kerry), Captain Slacke (Tipperary, Waterford and Kilkenny), H.A. Blake (Carlow, Queen's County, King's County, Kildare and Meath) and Captain Butler (Leitrim, Longford, Cavan and Westmeath). **94** The Midland Division, commanded by Captain Butler, at first covered Kildare, King's County, Westmeath, Meath, Cavan, Longford, Leitrim and Sligo; the Western Division, commanded by Assistant Inspector-General Andrew Reed, covered Galway, Mayo, Roscommon and Clare; the South-western Division, commanded by T.O. Plunkett, consisted of Cork, Kerry and Limerick; the South-eastern Division, commanded by Captain Slacke, covered Waterford, Kilkenny, Tipperary, Queen's County and Carlow. **95** The Northern Division, commanded by Assistant Inspector-General Francis N. Cullen, consisted of Antrim, Armagh, Belfast (which was regarded

tually phased out on 1 February 1898, and from 2 February the RIC county inspectors assumed responsibility for overseeing the work of the Crime Special Branch in their respective counties.

The Crime Branch Special Reports on agrarian crime and other secret society activity are an indispensable source for the historian of crime in the late nineteenth and early twentieth centuries. Most of them consist of monthly situation reports by Divisional Magistrates or Commissioners and county inspectors from February 1887 to January 1898, and by county inspectors and the inspector general of the RIC from February 1898 to July 1920 (although most of the reports deal with the period from February 1887 to February 1913) on the state of agrarian crime, incidence of evictions and boycotting, and the activities of illegal secret societies and suspected individuals and organisations such as the Gaelic Athletic Association, Gaelic League, United Irish League and the Ancient Order of Hibernians.[96] Much of the information on which these reports are based originally came from informers. Similar reports from the DMP 'G' or detective division are available in the National Archives of Ireland from January 1895 to February 1905. While the Crime Branch Special Reports may be consulted in cartons in the National Archives in Dublin, much of this material also found its way into the Colonial Office Records, Class CO 904, which are available in the National Archives, Kew (formerly the Public Record Office, Kew, London).[97] The Colonial Office files are discussed below.[98]

In addition to the monthly summaries which are filed in cartons, the researcher may consult the Crime Branch Special 'S' Files for the years 1890 to 1895, to which there is a separate card index in the National Archives of Ireland reading room. The subject matter of the 'S' files is similar to that of the main body of Crime Branch Special material. However, the 'S' files differ from the latter in that they consist of a series of reports on individual cases or suspects at a local level, rather than the general monthly situation reports relating to a county or a division that predominate in the main Crime Branch Special Reports. The light that the 'S' files throw on crime at local level is illustrated by such examples as CBS 1894 9129/S, a very large file of documents relating to the murder of Patrick Flahive at Heirhill, County Kerry on 30 August 1886 and the attempts to extradite one of the suspected murderers, Edward Kelly, from the United States; CBS 1894 9301/S, which contains the photographs and descriptions of numerous suspected individuals who were photographed surreptitiously;[99] and CBS 1893 7174A/S, a file documenting the methods used by the RIC to obtain a sample of handwriting from Martha Jane Vance of Bangor,

---

as a separate county for RIC operational purposes), Derry, Donegal, Down, Fermanagh, Louth, Monaghan and Tyrone. At the same time, Wicklow and Wexford were added to the South-eastern Division. **96** For a discussion of the work of the RIC intelligence gatherers in one county see Pádraig G. Lane, 'Government surveillance of subversion in Laois, 1890–1916' in Lane and Nolan (eds), *Laois history and society*, pp 601–25. **97** The National Archives, Kew, Richmond, Surrey TW9 4DU. **98** See p. 46. **99** CBS 1890 130/S documents the Special Branch's experiments with a number of different models of camera to obtain surreptitious photographs of suspects. CBS 1890 868/S details the methods of shadowing and observing suspects that were used by Special Branch officers at this period.

County Down, suspected of having procured drugs in order to perform an abortion on Sarah McGreevy, an unmarried domestic servant who died of a haemorrhage at Bangor as the result of an abortion in February 1892.

MANUSCRIPTS IN OTHER REPOSITORIES

One of the principal sources to consult outside of the National Archives of Ireland is the collection of Colonial Office Papers held in the National Archives, Kew. The relevant classes are CO 903 and Co 904. Most of the Crime Branch Special Monthly Reports discussed above may be found in the CO 904 material, but the latter source is more extensive than the National Archives of Ireland material for the early twentieth century. For instance, the National Archives of Ireland material contains no DMP 'G' division Crime Branch Special Reports on secret society activity in Dublin after February 1905, while the CO 904 Police Reports detail such activity down to 1914. The National Archives of Ireland Crime Branch Special Monthly Reports from the RIC cover the period down to February 1913 in considerable detail, but there is little material after this date – the exceptions being March 1914, March 1916, January, March and July 1917 and January, March and July 1920. In contrast, the CO 904 Reports include monthly confidential reports from the inspector generals and county inspectors down to September 1921. This material is available on microfilm in the National Library of Ireland[1] and in some Irish university libraries, as well as the National Archives, Kew. The CO 904 documents are essential for the historian researching such topics as the history of the IRB in the decade before the Easter Rising, illegal drilling by Unionists and the formation and development of the Ulster Volunteer Force in the 1911 to 1914 period, the growth of militant nationalism after the Easter Rebellion, the war between the IRA and the forces of the Crown from 1919 to 1921 and agrarian crime during the War of Independence period.[2]

The CO 903 series is a smaller collection of printed intelligence notes and police synopses of crime and outrage from 1887 to 1919, complementing the largely handwritten and much larger CO 904 series. Some of this material, for the years 1913 to 1916, has been published by Breandán Mac Giolla Choille as *Intelligence Notes, 1913–16* (Dublin, 1966).

The researcher who is interested in the history of the separatist movement from 1913 to 1921 will also find the holdings of the Bureau of Military History in Cathal Brugha Barracks, Dublin,[3] of considerable value. The largest single component of

---

[1] There is an index to the CO 904 papers at the National Library of Ireland enquiry desk. This material has been microfilmed as 'The British in Ireland' collection.   [2] For discussions of the latter topic see Paul Bew, 'Sinn Fein, agrarian radicalism and the War of Independence, 1919–1921' in D.G. Boyce (ed.), *The revolution in Ireland, 1879–1923* (Dublin, 1988), pp 217–34 and Tony Varley, 'Agrarian crime and social control: Sinn Féin and the land question in the West of Ireland in 1920' in Ciaran McCullagh, Mike Tomlinson and Tony Varley (eds), *Whose law and order? aspects of crime and social control in Irish society* (Dublin, 1988), pp 54–75.   [3] Bureau of Military History, Cathal Brugha Barracks, Rathmines, Dublin 6.

this material consists of some 1,773 written statements by members of the IRB, Irish Volunteers, IRA, Cumann na mBan, Fianna Éireann, Irish Citizen Army, RIC and DMP in which they relate their memories of this period, as well as written statements by other contemporaries, especially relations of people who were involved in these organisations. There are also some 334 sets of papers from participants in the struggle for independence and their opponents, and a small number of voice recordings.[4] Researchers should note, however, that due to space constrictions only a very small number of readers may consult this material at any one time, and that it is advisable to make an appointment up to two weeks in advance to secure a place in the Bureau's reading room.[5] Copies of the Bureau material are available for consultation in the National Archives of Ireland. A catalogue to this collection is available at the issue desk. There is also valuable material on the activities of the separatist movement in the Archives Department of University College Dublin.[6] This includes such important sources as Máire Comerford's unpublished memoirs, Liam Gaynor's account of his activities in the No. 1 Dungannon Club in Belfast, the IRB (he eventually rose to membership of the Supreme Council) and the Belfast Brigade of the IRA, and Sean Gaynor's account of his role as commandant of the First North Tipperary Brigade of the IRA. Ernie O'Malley's transcripts of approximately 400 interviews with veterans of the IRA and Cumann na mBan represent an especially important part of the U.C.D. manuscript collection.

Researchers will also find some useful material in the Manuscript Department of Trinity College Dublin. One may study the Irish Confederation's drift towards rebellion in 1848 by studying the reports supplied by a DMP detective who at one point acted as secretary to a branch of the organisation, and the reports of an informer who was also involved on the fringes of conspiratorial activity in Dublin in both 1848 and 1849.[7] The manuscript memoirs of David Harrel, who from 1859 served variously as a sub-inspector of constabulary, resident magistrate, under-secretary for Ireland and chief commissioner of the DMP, should be of particular interest to the historian of the Land War.[8] The Goulden Papers contain a wide range of material relating to the history of the RIC. Of particular interest is the barrack journal of the Coleraine constabulary from February 1838 to April 1839, as it contains brief details of the types of crimes and misdemeanours encountered by the

---

4 The voice recordings are of William T. Cosgrave, William O'Brien, George Gavan Duffy, Maud Gonne McBride, Seán T. O'Kelly, Kathleen Clarke, Seán Moylan, Seán Mac Eoin, Oscar Traynor, Áine Ceannt (the widow of Eamon Ceannt), Conor A. Maguire (a judge in the Dáil Éireann courts) and Joseph Martin (an engineer in the IRA's Meath Brigade in 1921). **5** For a guide to the Bureau's holdings see Conor Kostick, 'Mentioning the war: the Bureau of Military History' in *History Ireland*, 11, no. 2 (summer 2003), pp 43–47. **6** Archives Department, University College Dublin, Belfield, Dublin 4. **7** TCD MSS 2037–2040. For the Irish Confederation see Takashi Koseki, *Dublin Confederate Clubs and the Repeal movement* (Tokyo, 1992); William Nolan, 'The Irish Confederation in County Tipperary in 1848' in *Tipperary History* (1998), pp 2–18; Gary Owens, 'Popular mobilisation and the rising of 1848: the clubs of the Irish Confederation' in Laurence M. Geary (ed.), *Rebellion and remembrance in modern Ireland* (Dublin, 2001), pp 51–63. For an account of the little-known 1849 rebellion see Brendan Kiely, *The Waterford rebels of 1849* (Dublin, 1999). **8** TCD MS. 3918a.

constabulary of that town on a daily basis.⁹ There is a similar journal for the Carndonagh police district in County Donegal from November 1833 to May 1836 in the Public Record Office of Northern Ireland.¹⁰ Another important constabulary document is Inspector-General Brownrigg's confidential report on the state of Ireland in 1863, held by the National Library of Ireland. In this manuscript, Brownrigg outlines the extent of serious crime, including the activities of various secret societies, throughout Ireland: this is of particular interest to the historian of Fenianism at local level.¹¹

Another resource that the researcher may find useful is folklore. The Department of Irish Folklore at University College Dublin is the principal repository of folklore. It holds the manuscript collection of the Irish Folklore Commission, founded in 1935 to collect, preserve and study Irish folklore on a wide variety of topics. The subject of crime, particularly relating to faction fighting and the Land War, occurs frequently in the manuscripts held at UCD. One should treat such evidence with caution, as the folklore may be vague (either by design, or because of the passage of time between the occurrences described and when they were recorded) on such details as the timing of the incidents described, and sometimes strict historical accuracy may be sacrificed in the interests of telling a good story. Other factors that may affect the quality of the information recorded in folklore include the cultural and social values of the informant, the latter's conscious or subconscious defence of private or community interests, and the fact that the questions posed by the interviewer may influence the answer elicited from an informant.¹² Nevertheless folklore may, when approached with care, be studied to good effect by the historian of crime, as illustrated by Éanna Hickey's work on popular attitudes to the legal system in nineteenth-century Ireland, Mary Helen Thuente's discussion of popular attitudes to violence in pre-Famine Ireland, Cathal Póirtéir's folklore-based examination of crime during the Famine and Séamas MacPhilib's use of folklore to study the life and murder of Lord Leitrim, respectively.¹³

PARLIAMENTARY PAPERS

British parliamentary papers constitute one of the most useful published sources for the local historian investigating crime in nineteenth- and early twentieth-century

9 TCD MS. 7367. 10 PRONI, T.3711. 11 MS. 915, 'Report on the state of Ireland in the year 1863'. 12 Éanna Hickey, *Irish law and lawyers in modern folk tradition* (Dublin, 1999), pp 3, 5. See also Paul Thompson, *The voice of the past: oral history* (Oxford, 1978) on the usefulness and problems of oral history evidence. 13 Hickey, *Irish law and lawyers*, passim; Mary Helen Thuente, 'Violence in pre-Famine Ireland: the testimony of Irish folklore and fiction' in *Irish University Review*, xv (1985), pp 129–47; Cathal Póirtéir, *Famine echoes* (Dublin, 1995), pp 68–84; Séamas MacPhilib, 'Profile of a landlord in folk tradition and in contemporary accounts – the third earl of Leitrim' in *Ulster Folklife*, 34 (1998), pp 26–40. The evidence of popular songs and street ballads may also be of interest for the light that they throw on popular attitudes to crime. See Georges-Denis Zimmermann, *Songs of Irish rebellion: Irish political street ballads and rebel songs, 1780–1900* (Dublin, 1967).

Ireland.[14] A number of guides to this material may be consulted. The following indexes are available at the issue desk at the National Library of Ireland: *General index to the accounts and papers, reports of commissioners, estimates &c &c. printed by order of the House of Commons, or presented by command: 1801–1852* HC 1854 (0.10) lxxv 1; *General index to the bills, reports, estimates, accounts and papers, presented by order of the House of Commons, and to the papers presented by command, 1852–53–1868–69* HC 1870 (469–I) lxxi 1; *General index to the bills, reports, estimates, accounts and papers, printed by order of the House of Commons, and to the papers presented by command 1870–1878–79* HC 1880 (140) lxxxiii 1; *General alphabetical index to the bills, reports, estimates, accounts, and papers, presented by order of the House of Commons, and to the papers presented by command, 1880–89* HC 1889 (354) lxxxix 1; *General alphabetical index to the bills, reports, estimates, accounts and papers, presented by order of the House of Commons, and to the papers presented by command, 1890–1899* HC 1904 (368) cxii 1; and *General index to the bills, reports, and papers presented by order of the House of Commons and to the reports and papers presented by command 1900 to 1948–49* (London, 1960). These indexes are used when ordering copies of the original, printed parliamentary papers in the National Library and are the best published finding aid available.[15]

Some researchers may prefer to use Chadwyck-Healey's microfiche collection of parliamentary papers, complete sets of which are available in the National Library and the British Library. Researchers should consult Peter Cockton, *House of Commons parliamentary papers, 1801–1900: guide to the Chadwyck-Healey microfiche edition* (Cambridge, 1991) for general guidance on how to use this collection, and volume four of Cockton's *Subject catalogue of the House of Commons parliamentary papers, 1801–1900* (Cambridge, 1988) for details of the parliamentary papers relating to Ireland. Another alternative is to use the Enhanced Parliamentary Papers on Ireland 1801–1922 (EPPI) internet database, which includes a subject or 'bibliographical' search facility and aims to provide the complete text of Irish-related parliamentary papers on-line. The subject search facility provides full details of the titles of parliamentary papers, their session, volume and page numbers and, in many instances, abstracts of the contents.[16]

The types of parliamentary papers that are most interesting are the reports of royal commissions of inquiry or select committees, and annual returns of crime and outrage or other crime returns and copies of official correspondence relating to crime and outrage that were frequently requested by members of parliament. Royal commissions of inquiry were appointed by royal warrant to investigate a particular problem, and consisted of a number of persons who were considered to have expert knowledge on the subject under investigation. They differed from select commit-

---

14 For a brief but very useful discussion see Joseph Canning, '19th-century British parliamentary papers as a source for local history' in *Ulster Local Studies*, 11, no. 1 (summer 1989), pp 5–9. See also W.B. Stephens, *Sources for English local history* (Cambridge, 1981), pp 16–20. **15** Other relevant guides are P. and G. Ford, *Select list of British parliamentary papers, 1833–1899* (Oxford, 1953); A. and J. Maltby, *Ireland in the nineteenth century: a breviate of official publications* (Oxford, 1979). **16** The EPPI bibliographic database may be searched at www.eppi.ac.uk.

tees in that one did not have to be a member of parliament to be a commissioner, and their investigations and deliberations could last for more than one sitting of parliament. They usually interrogated numerous witnesses at several sessions, and reported their findings and recommendations in a printed report to parliament. Select committees were limited in the length of time in which they could operate – they could not conduct business when parliament was not in session, and their term expired at the end of the parliamentary session. Select committees consisted of cross-party representatives who could, under parliamentary powers and privilege, compel witnesses to attend and give evidence.[17] As with royal commissions of inquiry, select committees presented their findings and recommendations in printed form to parliament. Although the terms of reference and the constitution of royal commissions of inquiry and select committees might differ somewhat, their modes of procedure and the type of evidence that they produced were similar. For the local historian, the minutes of evidence taken during their sittings are of greatest interest. These minutes are usually indexed, which considerably facilitates their use. As crime and outrage were frequently the subject of their investigations, these parliamentary papers are therefore of particular interest to the historian trying to piece together a picture of crime at local level. This is not to say that these are entirely unproblematic sources, however. For instance, it was not unknown for commissioners and members of select committees to ask leading questions of witnesses, which coloured the tone of their proceedings and the content of the evidence that was given to them. Despite this feature of many parliamentary papers, they remain an especially valuable resource for the local historian.[18]

A close study of two typical investigations into crime and outrage illustrates the potential that this type of parliamentary paper offers the researcher, as well as some problems that the researcher should be aware of. The first is *Report from the select comittee on outrages (Ireland); with proceedings of the committee, minutes of evidence, appendix and index* HC 1852 (438) xiv 1. It was called to investigate the alarming upsurge in agrarian and other crime in parts of counties Armagh, Monaghan and Louth in the late 1840s and early 1850s.[19] The committee examined fourteen witnesses over

---

17 Peter Cockton, *House of Commons parliamentary papers, 1801–1900: guide to the Chadwyck-Healey microfiche collection* (Cambridge, 1991), p. 14. **18** For examples of secondary sources that rely heavily on parliamentary papers see Kevin B. Nowlan, 'Agrarian unrest in Ireland, 1800–1845' in *University Review*, 2, no. 6, pp 7–16; Charles Dillon, 'The burning of Anahagh, 1830' in *Dúiche Néill*, 1, no. 1 (1986), pp 22–61; idem, 'The wrecking of Maghery, County Armagh, 1830' in *Dúiche Néill*, 1, no. 2 (1987), pp 107–30. **19** The violence in the region in the 1835 to 1855 period, which saw three sectarian murders, fourteen agrarian murders and three attempted murders, and eight other murders are discussed in Kevin McMahon and Thomas McKeown, 'Agrarian disturbance around Crossmaglen, 1835–1855: part I' in *Seanchas Ard Mhacha*, 9, no. 2 (1979), pp 302–32; idem, 'Agrarian disturbances around Crossmaglen, 1835–1855: part II' in *Seanchas Ard Mhacha*, 9, no. 1 (1980–81), pp 149–75; idem, 'Agrarian disturbances around Crossmaglen, 1835–1855: part III' in *Seanchas Ard Mhacha*, 9, no. 2 (1982), pp 380–416; idem, 'Agrarian disturbances around Crossmaglen, 1835–1855: part IV' in *Seanchas Ard Mhacha*, 11, no. 2 (1985), pp 342–62; idem, 'Agrarian disturbances around Crossmaglen, 1835–1855: part V' in *Seanchas Ard Mhacha*, 12, no. 1 (1986), pp 213–50; Kevin McMahon and Rory Kieran, 'Agrarian disturbances

SELECT COMMITTEE ON OUTRAGES (IRELAND).   185

the desperate Rascal, he had better watch and prayr for if all police in Ireland were watching him, he will go the road, for Hell is yawning for him long since. We will send him to Fiddler's Green. It is long since he should have got it; there is an Establishment 'in Jonesboro' that will soon be set flames to. It will take Whipper in McDonald to never sleep, and to hell with all the Police of Ireland. We will send all who wears the cloyth to Blazes. Hell is open for Crawford.

H. J. Brownrigg, Esq.

30 April 1852.

I am, General Vengeance."

1927. Who is "Bumper Squire Jones"?—A magistrate of the county.

1928. Who is "Crawford"?—A sub-inspector. I also produce a threatening notice served on Mr. Coulter; who was murdered.

1929. Also in the county of Louth?—In the county of Armagh.

1930. Near Crossmaglen?—Yes.

[*The Witness delivered in the following document, which was read:*]

Take notice, that the man who shot at those men vos not the fool to lave himself in any one's power to convict him, so do not be mistaken, i will not give up the job, i will put in a Better charge the next time, i did not wish to cill them that time, But let them remember if the do not give up the lands the have taken above and below it will be as it was with Jack McGuine's, he got a good advice, but he did not take it this is no Scholby's Play, their names went true the country.

Thomas McAide Roach,

Saml. Coulter Mounthill.

James Quigley Roach,

do not let them Be blaming each other, McAidle is woss than any of them, the two Countys is up agin them, let no man take a poor man's land.

Posted on the door of one James Donelly, over the proclamation offering a reward of 80 *l.*, in the case of the murderous attack on Mr. Saml. Coulter in Feb. 1849, (rather more than two years before Mr. C.'s murder).

1931. Have you any other notice?—A threatening notice

0.38.   A A   which

4   Extract from *Report from the select committee on outrages (Ireland)* ... HC 1852 (438) xiv 1.

seventeen days, from 22 March to 28 May, 1852. The witnesses examined were Captain Bartholomew Warburton, a stipendiary magistrate based in Forkhill; Captain George Fitzmaurice, a resident magistrate in Crossmaglen; Edward Golding, a justice of the peace in County Monaghan for twelve years and a land agent who replaced Thomas Bateson, the land agent for Lord Templeton who was murdered in December 1851; Henry John Brownrigg, the inspector general of the Irish Constabulary; Maxwell Hamilton, crown solicitor for the north-east circuit with some twenty-one years' experience in the post; John Hatchell, the attorney general for Ireland; James Major, the assistant barrister for County Monaghan and chairman of Monaghan quarter sessions; Fr James McMeel, parish priest of Castleblayney; Fr Michael Lennon, parish priest of Upper Creggan; Burton Brabazon, who had served for eleven years as sub-sheriff for County Louth; William Kirk, a linen merchant and bleacher from Annvale, near Keady, and a justice of the peace for County Armagh; James O'Callaghan, who was a justice of the peace for County Armagh and Monaghan for forty-six years, and for County Louth for sixteen years; the Reverend Daniel Gun Brown, the Presbyterian minister for Newtownhamilton parish for nineteen years; and Sir Matthew Barrington, crown solicitor for the Munster circuit for thirty-six years. With the exceptions of Hatchell, Brownrigg and Barrington, these men had an intimate knowledge of the disturbed district, and one can assume that the other witnesses were interrogated due to their general professional familiarity with cases of agrarian crime. To an extent, the evidence is coloured by the personal prejudices and mindsets peculiar to the witnesses' occupations, a factor which the researcher has to be careful about when using these sources. For example, the inspector general makes alarmist claims about the existence of a widespread, oath-bound 'Ribbon' conspiracy in the district, which is not untypical of the mindset of policemen, magistrates and other contemporaries when they discussed agrarian crime in this period, although tangible evidence for the existence of such an organisation is thin on the ground.[20] More usefully, Brownrigg supplied copies of various threatening letters that had been posted in the area, which the committee reproduced in its report. When it came to describing Thomas

around Crossmaglen, 1835–1855: part VI' in *Seanchas Ard Mhacha*, xii, no. 2 (1987), pp 194–250; Kevin McMahon, 'Agrarian disturbances around Crossmaglen, 1835–1855: part VII' in *Seanchas Ard Mhacha*, 13, no. 2 (1989), pp 167–229. See also *A return of the number of murders and waylayings in the baronies of Upper and Lower Fews, in the county of Armagh, during the six years, 1844 to 1850; also, copies of the depositions taken by the coroner of Armagh county, at the inquest held on the body of the late Mr Mauleverer* HC 1850 (566) li 517 and *A return of the number of murders, waylayings, assaults, threatening notices, incendiary fires, or other crimes of an agrarian nature, reported by the constabulary within the counties of Louth, Armagh, and Monaghan, since 1 Jan. 1849; distinguishing by name the persons murdered and waylaid; whether informations have been sworn in the case, and the result of any trial of the same* HC 1852 (448) xlvii 465. **20** For a sceptical view of these claims see Vaughan, *Landlords and tenants in mid-Victorian Ireland*, pp 189–202. The epithet of 'Ribbonmen', which, properly speaking, was the designation of a secret, hierarchical, Catholic-nationalist, sectarian and largely urban secret society which existed in parts of Ulster and Leinster in the pre-Famine period, was often erroneously applied to agrarian secret societies. Brownrigg's evidence to the select committee in 1852 is a good example of this conflation. For discussions of the non-agrarian Ribbonmen see Tom Garvin, 'Defenders, Ribbonmen and others: underground political networks in

Bateson, the murdered land agent, some of the witnesses had rather different opinions to offer. James Major, responding to a question about whether he had heard that Bateson had 'irritated the people very much by continually shooting their dogs', responded that

> Mr Bateson was a most humane man, and most considerate towards the tenantry; and not only so, but I can speak from judicial knowledge, that during a period of nearly five years – he had been in the country after I was there, and I have taken some pains to ascertain it – there were only 36 or 37 ejectments over a most extensive estate brought into my court. I took some pains to enquire into it in consequence of some observations which were made. There was not, in the county of Monaghan, a single landowner or agent who came into my court less frequently than Mr Bateson.

Fr McMeel, who was sympathetic to the Tenant League, offered quite a different picture of Bateson. In McMeel's view, Bateson was 'a harsh man in his manner', who 'exacted high rents very harshly' and spoke in an 'unkindly' manner to the peasantry, who allegedly expressed the view that if Bateson had not been killed '[W]e should all have been tyrannised over, or all have been put out'. This conflicting evidence illustrates the caution that is needed when reading parliamentary papers: while they are certainly an important source for the historian of crime, one needs to weigh up carefully conflicting evidence and search for evidence of bias or evasion and possible explanations for this bias and evasion, and one should also endeavour to use other contemporary sources in order to try and gain a more complete picture of factors behind the crimes under discussion.

Westmeath, and parts of Longford, Meath and King's County, saw a similar crime wave in the late 1860s and early 1870s to that experienced by parts of counties Armagh, Monaghan and Louth in the late 1840s and early 1850s. As in the more northerly district, the later outbreak prompted the setting up of a select committee to enquire into reasons behind the disturbances. Its evidence may be studied in *Report from the select committee on Westmeath, &c (unlawful combinations); together with the proceedings of the committee, minutes of evidence, and appendix* HC 1871 (147) xiii 547. The select committee sat for eight days, from 13 March to 30 March 1871, interviewing fourteen witnesses in the process. As was almost always the case with royal commissions of inquiry or select committees into crime and outrage in Ireland, the investigators in this instance called on pillars of the community for explanations of why crimes were being committed. This skewed perspective is a factor that the researcher should take into account when assessing the evidence that these parliamentary bodies produced. There is no testimony from the actual perpetrators of crime in these sources: the closest that one gets to first-hand evidence from them

---

pre-Famine Ireland' in *Past & Present*, no. 96 (1982), pp 133–55; M.R. Beames, 'The Ribbon societies: lower-class nationalism in pre-Famine Ireland' in *Past & Present*, no. 97 (1982), pp 128–43.

is in the form of threatening letters or notices. The witnesses who were examined in 1871 were Captain George Talbot, a resident magistrate of eighteen years' service, almost eight of them in Westmeath; William Morris Reade, a resident magistrate based in Kilbeggan; Captain William Fitzjames Barry, another Westmeath magistrate who had previously served in Mayo, Waterford and Roscommon; Ralph Smith Cusack, chairman of the Midland Great Western Railway Company; George Augustus Rochfort-Boyd, deputy lieutenant of the county for more than thirty years; Reverend James Crofton of Dunleer, County Louth, who was trustee for a property in Westmeath for his children and his sister-in-law; William Mooney, clerk of the crown for Westmeath; Stephen Seed, senior crown solicitor for Meath and Kildare; John Julian, crown solicitor for Westmeath and King's County; Dr Thomas Nulty, Catholic bishop of Meath; Joseph Henry Lyttelton, a resident magistrate at Tullamore, whose district bordered Westmeath; Norman Lionel Townsend, sub-inspector of Kilbeggan district; Colonel Sir John Stewart-Wood, inspector general of the RIC; and Colonel Fitzstephen French, MP for Roscommon. These men were chosen as witnesses because of their familiarity with Westmeath – Ralph Smith Cusack's inclusion may be explained by the fact that one of his employees, the stationmaster at Mullingar, was murdered in March 1869,[21] and the select committee undoubtedly believed that he could give valuable evidence about the circumstances surrounding the killing. One of the striking features of the evidence from this select committee is that even stronger claims were made about the existence of a powerful 'Ribbon' conspiracy than were made in the 1852 select committee discussed above – particularly, but not only, by Stephen Seed. Historian A.C. Murray shows how a careful reading of even such lurid testimony as is offered by many of the Westmeath select committee witnesses can reveal a more plausible picture of crime and its causes. He argues strongly that one should discount police and magistrate accounts of 'Ribbonism' being behind agrarian crime, and suggests that one should instead pay closer attention to the less sensationalist details offered by witnesses to select committees. He explains why the police authorities often persisted in attributing agrarian crime to the supposed existence of Ribbonism:

> The answer that most readily suggests itself is that the terms Ribbonism, Ribbonman, and Ribbon society were labels affixed by the police and magistrates to crimes they could not solve, criminals they could not catch, and gangs they could not break up. The phenomenon of Ribbonism, as defined by the authorities, was an illusion created by their failure to maintain law and order in the countryside. To blame their almost complete failure to apprehend agrarian criminals, most notably murderers, upon the Ribbon society in part absolved both the local and central authorities, excused the incompetence and apathy of the majority of the magistrates and the inad-

---

[21] See *Copies of the resolutions and suggestions made at a meeting of the magistrates called by the vice lieutenant of Westmeath county, called after the murder of Mr Anketell, station master at Mullingar* HC 1868–69 (215) li 413.

equate and inefficient police methods which were designed to prevent and put down a rising rather than prevent and detect crime, while at the same time enabling officials to plead for extraordinary measures in order to deal with agrarian crime in the county.[22]

One can, then, discount or at least be very sceptical of contemporary claims that a highly organised Ribbon system, with passwords, secret handshakes, parish masters and county delegates was behind agrarian crime in Westmeath in this period (or, indeed, in other areas at other periods). Murray shows that there is sufficient evidence of a more mundane but plausible kind in the Westmeath select committee's report to explain the incidence of violence in the county.[23]

The royal commissions of inquiry and select committees form an invaluable source for the study of crime in Ireland throughout the Union period. What follows is merely an indicative selection of this vast corpus of material. For the disturbed decade after the ending of the Napoleonic Wars, the most important sources are

- *Minutes of evidence taken before the select committee appointed to inquire into the disturbances in Ireland, in the last session of parliament, 13 May–18 June 1824* HC 1825 (20) vii 1;
- *Minutes of evidence taken before the select committee of the House of Lords appointed to examine the nature and extent of the disturbances which have prevailed in those districts of Ireland which are now subject to the provisions of the Insurrection Act, and to report to the House, 18 May–23 June 1824* HL 1825 (200) vii 501;
- *Minutes of evidence taken before the select committee of the House of Lords appointed to inquire into the state of Ireland, more particularly with reference to the circumstances which may have led to disturbances in that part of the United Kingdom* HL 1825 (181) ix 1.

For the Tithe War of the 1830s and other disturbances in that decade, the most important parliamentary investigations are

- *Report from the select committee appointed to take into consideration the state of the poorer classes in Ireland, relative to the state of the country, as exemplified by the criminal returns* HC 1830 (667) vii 1;
- *Report from the select committee appointed to examine into the state of the disturbed counties in Ireland, into the immediate causes which have produced the same, and into the efficiency of the laws for the suppression of outrages against the public peace* HC 1831–32 (677) xvi 1;
- *Minutes of evidence taken before the select committee of the House of Lords appointed to inquire into the state of Ireland since 1835, in respect of crime and outrage, which have rendered life and property insecure in that part of the empire, and to report to the House* HL 1839 486–I 486–II xi 1.423.

22 A.C. Murray, 'Agrarian violence and nationalism in nineteenth-century Ireland: the myth of Ribbonism' in *Irish Economic and Social History*, 13 (1986), p. 71.   23 Ibid., pp 56–73.

The royal commissions of inquiry and select committees did not only enquire into agrarian disturbances. They also investigated such illegal activity as poteen-making, the violence that frequently accompanied general elections and by-elections, and other outbreaks of violence in towns and cities. The researcher interested in the history of illicit distillation will find the following reports particularly interesting:

- *Report from the select committee appointed to inquire into the alleged increase and extent of illicit distillation in Ireland, and into the means for the prevention thereof* HC 1812–13 (269) 1;
- *Report from the select committee appointed to inquire into the causes and extent of illicit distillation of spirits in Ireland, and into the means for the prevention thereof, and into the operation and effects of the laws and regulations created for the suppression thereof* HC 1816 (436) ix 9;
- *Second report from select committee on illicit distillation in Ireland: with an appendix of minutes and evidence* HC 1816 (490) ix 13;
- *Report from the select committee of the House of Lords, appointed to consider the consequences of extending the functions of the constabulary in Ireland to the suppression or prevention of illicit distillation; and to report thereon to the House; together with the minutes of evidence, and an appendix and index* HL 1854 (53) x 1.[24]

The parliamentary investigations of electoral violence, as K. Theodore Hoppen has shown,[25] are indispensable sources for studying this aspect of crime and disorder in Irish towns and cities. Representative examples include

- *Minutes of evidence taken before the select committee on the Waterford county election petition; with the proceedings and index* HC 1867 (205) viii 285
- *Minutes of evidence taken at the trial of the Drogheda election petition (1869)* HC 1868–69 (27) xlix 497.

Sectarian tensions in nineteenth-century Belfast occasionally escalated into communal riots, the most serious of which occurred in 1857, 1864 and 1886. These may be studied in detail in

- *Report of the commissioners of inquiry into the origin and character of the riots in Belfast in July and September 1857; together with minutes of evidence and appendix* HC 1857–58 [2309] xxvi 1;

---

24 For a discussion of illegal manufacture of spirits see K.H. Connell, 'Illicit distillation' in K.H. Connell, *Irish peasant society: four historical essays* (Oxford, 1968), pp 1–50; Norma M. Dawson, 'Illicit distillation and the Revenue Police in Ireland in the eighteenth and nineteenth centuries' in *Irish Jurist*, xii, new series, part 2 (winter 1977), pp 289–94. See also *Accounts of the number of detections, and number of persons prosecuted, convicted, and confined in the several gaols of Ireland, for any offence against the laws for the suppression of illicit distillation, 1800 to 1852* HC 1852–53 (547) xcix 549.   **25** K. Theodore Hoppen, *Elections, politics, and society in Ireland, 1832–1885* (Oxford, 1984).

- *Report of the commissioners of inquiry, 1864, respecting the magisterial and police arrangements and establishments of the borough of Belfast* HC 1865 [3466] xxviii 1;
- *Minutes of evidence and appendix to the report of the commissioners of inquiry, 1864, respecting the borough of Belfast* HC 1865 [3466–I] xxviii 27;
- *Belfast riots commission, 1886. Report of the Belfast riots commissioners. Minutes of evidence, and appendix* HC 1887 (c.4925) xviii 1.[26]

The widespread disturbances arising from the Dublin lock–out dispute in 1913 are documented in

- *Report of the Dublin disturbances commission* HC 1914 Cd, 7269 xviii 513; and
- *Appendix to report of the Dublin disturbances commission. Minutes of evidence and appendices* HC 1914 Cd. 7272 xviii 533.[27]

The events of the 1916 Rising are detailed in

- *Report of the royal commission on the rebellion in Ireland* HC 1916 Cd 8279 xi 171 and
- *Report of the royal commission on the rebellion in Ireland: evidence and appendix* HC 1916 Cd 8311 xi 185.

Another important type of parliamentary paper is the official return containing statistical and other details of crime, or copies of the official correspondence relating to specific crimes. From 1863 annual crime returns for the entire country, known as judicial statistics, were compiled annually by the RIC and DMP, and in the 1870s and 1880s the RIC also supplied statistical details of the number of agrarian outrages and boycotting. In addition to these regular returns of nation-wide crime, Dublin Castle was also often required to produce returns on an irregular basis that referred to specific criminal incidents or to crime in specific localities, following a request for this information by a member of parliament. These were often requests for copies of official correspondence concerning specific criminal incidents. The parliamentary papers that were produced in response to requests from members of parliament are of particular interest to the local historian.

Examples of returns of official correspondence concerning crime in the pre-Famine and Famine periods include

---

26 See also Andrew Boyd, *Holy war in Ireland* (Tralee, 1972); Sybil E. Baker, 'Orange and green: Belfast, 1832–1912' in H.J. Dyos and Michael Wolff (eds), *The Victorian city: images and realities* (2 vols, London, 1973), ii, pp 789–814; and Catherine Hirst, *Religion, politics and violence in nineteenth-century Belfast: the Pound and Sandy Row* (Dublin, 2002). For sectarian rioting in Derry see *Report of the commissioners of inquiry, 1869, into the riots and disturbances in the city of Londonderry. With minutes of evidence and appendix* HC 1870 (c.5) xxxii 411. The bloodiest rural affray in Ulster in the nineteenth century is the subject of *Papers relating to an investigation held at Castlewellan into the occurrences at Dolly's Brae, on the 12th of July, 1849* HC 1850 [1143] li 331. **27** For an exhaustive account of the lock-out dispute see Pádraig Yeates, *Lockout: Dublin 1913* (Dublin, 2000).

- *Papers relating to the nature and extent of disturbances in Ireland* HC 1816 (479) ix 567;
- *Papers relating to disturbances in the county of Louth* HC 1817 (263) viii 491;
- *Correspondence and documents relative to the state of the Queen's County* HC 1831–32 (in 677) xvi 543;
- *Papers relating to the proclamation of baronies in the county of Westmeath* HC 1834 (292) xlvii 363;
- *Copies of the several documents on which the baronies of Ballyboy, Ballybrit, Eglish and Garrycastle in the King's County, were declared to be in a state of disturbance and insubordination* HC 1834 (241) xlvii 16;
- *Copy of the report of the investigation held at Portadown on the 10th April 1834, and subsequent days into the conduct of Chief Constable of Police Brennan, and the result; also, copy of letter from Chief Constable Brennan to Sub-inspector of Police Henry, at Armagh, upon the subject of the disturbance which took place in the town of Portadown upon the Easter Monday preceding* HC 1835 (258) xlv 527;
- *Copies or extracts from reports from magistrates or officers of the constabulary, to his majesty's government, with reference to riotous proceedings which lately took place in the village of Ballykelly, parish of Tamlaght-finlagan, in the county of Londonderry* HC 1835 (345) xlv 489;
- *Extracts made by Colonel MacGregor from the police reports, stating the particulars of the principal homicides in Ireland, 1845–46, and forwarded to the Home Office by him* HC 1846 (179) xxxv 261.

The pre-Famine period saw periodic requests for detailed crime returns, such as:

- *Number and nature of offences reported to the government as having taken place in the county of Clare, 1831–32* HC 1833 (79) xxix 405;
- *Number of persons tried and found guilty or acquitted, 1832–33, in Clare, distinguishing the nature of each offence* HC 1833 (66) xxix 431;
- *Crimes and outrages reported by the stipendiary magistrates and officers of police in Ireland to the inspector-general of police, or to the Irish government, 1 January 1836 to 12 December 1837; distinguishing such crimes as were contained in the usual monthly reports, and such as were specially reported* HC 1837–38 (in 157) xlvi 427.

Such returns were made more frequently during the Famine years. This undoubtedly reflects the increased anxiety felt by British and Irish members of parliament and other contemporaries about the condition of Ireland at this period. Among the most revealing parliamentary papers dealing with crime during the Famine are

- *Names of persons, places, and nature of outrages, reported to the Constabulary Office, as occurring within the barony of Owenybeg, in the county of Limerick, 1845, 1846, both inclusive* HC 1846 (342) xxxv 459;
- *Abstracts of the police reports of some of the principal outrages in the counties of Tipperary, Limerick, Clare, Leitrim, and Roscommon* HC 1846 [710] xxxv 307;

- Return of aggravated assaults; of incendiary fires; robbery of arms; administration of unlawful oaths; threatening letters; malicious injuries to property; and, firing into dwellings, since 1845; specifying particulars in each case HC 1846 (369) xxxv 181;
- Return of all homicides that have been committed in Ireland since January 1846; specifying the county and the barony in which each homicide was committed; name and condition of person killed; rewards offered in each instance; instances in which claimed; number of convictions; attempts at murder, attended with bodily injuries or without HC 1846 (363) xxxv 273.[28]

Beginning in 1863, the RIC and DMP supplied parliament with annual statistics of crimes committed throughout all of Ireland.[29] The DMP had, since its formation in 1838, been publishing annual statistics of crimes committed within the area of its jurisdiction, although these were not produced as parliamentary papers.[30] From 1863 onwards the Dublin force produced these statistics, as well as furnishing slightly different returns that were published as part of the national crime statistics. The joint RIC–DMP crime returns, published as annual parliamentary papers, were referred to as the Irish judicial statistics. In the 1870s the RIC also made annual returns of agrarian crime for selected counties.[31] In 1880 the RIC provided a statistical breakdown of 'outrages' committed in every county, on a monthly basis, from 1844 to 1880, which was printed as a parliamentary return in 1881.[32] Thereafter, the force produced similar returns on a periodic basis which were published as parliamentary papers.[33] These returns are important for gauging the extent of agrarian crime in the 1880s and in the anti-grazier agitation of the early twentieth century. In the returns for 1882–85 and 1887–92, offences dealt with under the Prevention of Crimes (Ireland) Act of 1882 and the Criminal Law and Procedure (Ireland) Act of 1887 are not tabulated in the general returns of indictable crimes, but are listed elsewhere in the returns for these years. These give

---

28 The last-cited parliamentary paper may be used in conjunction with *A return of all murders that have been committed in Ireland since the 1st day of January 1842; specifying the county, and the barony of the county, where such murder had been committed; the name and condition of the person so murdered; also, a return of the rewards offered in each such instance; when the rewards have been claimed; and when conviction has followed; the different queries to be arranged in columns; similar return of attempts to murder, attended with bodily injuries, arranged in columns; similar return of attempts to murder, not attended with bodily injury, arranged in columns* HC 1846 (220) xxxv 293. **29** *Return of judicial statistics of Ireland, 1863* HC 1864 [3418] lvii 653. **30** *Statistical returns of the Dublin Metropolitan Police, 1838–1919* (Dublin, 1839–1920). These statistics were published annually under slightly varying titles. They may be consulted in the National Library (call number IR 3522 d 6). The volumes for 1851 and 1880 are missing. **31** For example, *Return of all arrests made under the Protection of Life and Property Act, 1871, since the passing of the Act, distinguishing the nature of offence; duration of imprisonment; county and parish* HC 1875 (180) lxii 183. **32** *Return of outrages reported to the Royal Irish Constabulary Office from 1 Jan. 1844 to 31 Dec. 1880* HC 1881 [c.2756] lxxvii 887. **33** See *Return of the number of agrarian offences in each county in Ireland reported to the Constabulary Office in each month in 1880, distinguishing offences against the person, offences against property, and offences against the public peace, with summary* HC 1881 (12) lxxvii 619; *Return of the number of agrarian offences in each county in Ireland reported to the Constabulary Office in 1881, distinguishing offences against the person, offences against property, and offences against the public peace, with summary* HC 1882 (8) lv 1.

county-by-county breakdowns of the numbers of people prosecuted for such agrarian offences as intimidation, riot or unlawful assembly, forcible possession of farms, assault on bailiffs or constables, being found at night under suspicious circumstances in a proclaimed district or being a stranger found under suspicious circumstances in a proclaimed district.[34]

Other useful returns in the 1880s include those detailing the number of Land League meetings in each county and the number of cases of resistance to police when they were protecting process servers and other officials,[35] and the number of boycotted people or people receiving special police protection in each county.[36] Similar returns of instances of boycotting and cattle driving were produced during the land agitation of the early twentieth century.[37] During the War of Independence, it was no longer possible for the RIC to produce this sort of detailed return of crime at local level, given the fact that the force was withdrawn from barracks throughout much of the country and, in some areas, people reported crimes and took cases to Republican courts and the IRA rather than the legally constituted authorities.[38] The force did, however, produce statistics of the political violence that occurred in 1919, in *Return showing, with dates, the number of murders of members of the Royal Irish Constabulary and of the Dublin Metropolitan Police,*

---

34 For a synopsis of the provisions of these Acts see Crossman, *Politics, law and order*, pp 224–27. **35** *Return showing, for each month of 1879 and 1880, the number of Land League meetings held and agrarian crimes reported to the inspector general of the Royal Irish Constabulary, in each county throughout Ireland* HC 1881 (5) lxxvii 793; *Return of all agrarian crimes and outrages reported by the Royal Irish Constabulary in the counties of Galway, Mayo, Sligo, and Donegal, from 1st February 1880 to 30th June 1880; number of meetings for promoting the land agitation reported by the constabulary within the same counties since 30th June 1879; number of cases reported by the constabulary in which resistance was offered to the police when protecting process servers, bailiffs, and others in the execution of their duty, &c* HC 1880 (327) lx 291. **36** *Return of the number of persons receiving special police protection in each county in Ireland on 31st December 1880* HC 1881 (1) lxxvi 641; *Return showing, by provinces and counties, the number of persons specially protected by the Royal Irish Constabulary on 31st July 1887 and 31st January 1888* HC 1888 [c.5309] lxxxviii 305. **37** *Return, by counties and quarterly periods, of the number of cattle-drives reported by the Royal Irish Constabulary to have taken place in Ireland from 1st January 1907 to 30th September 1908* HC 1908 (310) xc 3; *Return showing for each month of 1908 the number of cattle-drives, cases of firing into houses and at persons, of boycotting (complete and partial), prosecutions for foregoing offences, and results of prosecutions, claims for malicious injuries, amount of awards, appeals against awards, &c* HC 1908 (289) xc 89; *Return of the number of cases of boycotting throughout Ireland on certain dates in the years 1893–1909 inclusive, with notes on the issue of proclamations under the Criminal Law and Procedure Act, 1887, and the dates in 1901 when proceedings were first instituted under the same Act* HC 1909 (116) lxxiii 7; *Return showing the number of persons in Ireland returned as boycotted during the four years ended the 31st December, 1909, who have been, in addition, the victims of overt crime, and indicating the acts of outrage in each case, without specifying the names of the individuals attacked* HC 1910 (93) lxxvi 111. For discussions of the land agitation in this period see Paul Bew, *Conflict and conciliation in Ireland 1890–1910: Parnellites and radical agrarians* (Oxford, 1987); David Seth Jones, *Graziers, land reform, and political reform in Ireland* (Washington, D.C., 1995). **38** For the operation of the Republican courts see James Casey, 'Republican courts in Ireland, 1919–22' in *Irish Jurist*, v (1970), pp 321–42; Mary Kotsonouris, *Retreat from revolution: the Dáil courts, 1920–24* (Dublin, 1994); Raé Kearns, 'Republican justice in Meath 1919–1922' in *Ríocht na Midhe*, ix, no. 2 (1996), pp 154–63; and F.J. Costello, 'The Republican courts and the decline of British rule in Ireland, 1919–1921' in *Éire-Ireland*, xxv, no. 2 (summer 1990), pp 36–55.

and of soldiers, civilians, and the number of political outrages on persons and property in Ireland since 1st January 1919 HC 1920 (63) xl 799, and produced similar returns of political violence over shorter periods thereafter.[39]

The judicial statistics and returns of outrages allow the researcher to build up a detailed picture of crime at local level for each year. The judicial statistics are divided into tables that show the number and type of indictable offences (which were tried before a jury) and non-indictable offences (which were tried summarily by magistrates) committed annually in each county. The indictable offences are tabled in six sub-sections: offences against the person (which includes murder, attempted murder, manslaughter, rape, concealing births, assaults inflicting bodily harm, and assaults on policemen), offences against property with violence (which mainly consists of burglary offences), offences against property without violence, malicious offences against property (which includes arson, killing and maiming cattle, and sending letters threatening to burn houses or otherwise harm property), forgery and other currency offences, and miscellaneous offences (including rioting and attempting to commit suicide). The non-indictable offences, which always heavily out-numbered indictable offences, are tabled alphabetically, beginning with aggravated assaults on women and children and finishing with offences against the Weights and Measures Act. The most numerous non-indictable offences tend to be drunkenness or being drunk and disorderly, offences against the Highway Act (which usually meant allowing pigs, cattle or other animals to wander onto the

---

39 These returns are not always complete. For example, the *Return showing the number of serious outrages in Ireland reported by the Royal Irish Constabulary and the Dublin Metropolitan Police for the months of May and June, 1920* covers the period from 8 May to 26 June inclusive. It details the instances of courthouses destroyed or damaged and unsuccessful attacks on courthouses, the destruction or damage of occupied or unoccupied RIC barracks and unsuccessful attacks on police barracks, raids on coastguard stations, raids on other government buildings (including post offices), attacks on the mail, raids for arms, raids for petrol, thefts of old age pensions, firing into private dwelling houses, incendiary fires and arson, policemen killed and injured, soldiers killed and injured, soldiers disarmed, civilians killed and injured and intimidation. However, it does not include the 20 civilians killed in riots in Derry in the period. The Return showing the number of serious outrages in Ireland reported by the Royal Irish Constabulary and the Dublin Metropolitan Police during the months of July, August and September, 1920, which covers the period from 3 July to 2 October, 1920 contains similar information to the above source, as well as giving details of the number of kidnappings in the period. It does not, however, include details of the destruction caused in sectarian riots in Ulster, or during police and military reprisals at 'Tuam, Mallow, Balbriggan, &c' in these months, nor details of the number civilians killed in the sectarian clashes or the police and military reprisals. For a recent discussion of one of the most notorious reprisal incidents of this year see Tim Carey and Marcus de Búrca, 'Bloody Sunday 1920: new evidence' in *History Ireland*, 11, no. 2 (summer 2003), pp 10–16. The researcher who is interested in police casualties during the Easter Rising and War of Independence will find a useful database in Jim Herlihy, *The Royal Irish Constabulary: a short history and genealogical guide, with a select list of medal awards and casualties* (Dublin, 1997) and idem, *The Dublin Metropolitan Police: a short history and genealogical guide* (Dublin, 2001), pp 172–81. See also Richard Abbott, *Police casualties in Ireland, 1919–1922* (Cork and Dublin, 2000), and W.J. Lowe, 'The war against the RIC, 1919–21' in *Éire-Ireland*, xxxvii, nos 3 and 4 (autumn/winter 2002), pp 79–117.

public road) and common assaults. A useful feature of the judicial statistics is that they give a county-by-county breakdown of the number of 'known depredators, offenders, and suspected persons at large' within each police district. The returns specify whether these are 'known thieves and depredators', receivers of stolen goods, prostitutes, 'suspected persons', or vagrants and tramps. Each police district also details the number of 'houses of bad character', such as the houses of receivers of stolen goods, brothels and 'houses of ill-fame', tramps' lodging houses, and public houses, beer shops, coffee shops and other suspected houses to which thieves and prostitutes resorted in the locality.

While there is no doubt that these parliamentary returns of crime are of immense value to the researcher, a cautionary note should be sounded about interpreting this material. As V.A.C. Gatrell and T.B. Hadden have argued in their essay on the crime statistics of nineteenth-century England and Wales, crime statistics do not necessarily reflect the true incidence of crime: instead, they reflect police knowledge of crime, which is not the same thing. Furthermore, the statistics reflect such variables as changes in the numbers of police, and administrative and legal changes which led to different levels of intensity of law-and-order enforcement over the course of the century.[40] One can use the insights gained from Gatrell and Hadden's analysis of English and Welsh crime statistics to interpret the Irish crime statistics. In Ireland, which was much more heavily policed than England and Wales throughout this period, the proportionately higher incidence of such offences as assaults on police officers may be read in two ways: the police were either much more unpopular in Ireland than in England and Wales, as is evidenced by the crime returns, or the higher incidence of police assaults in Ireland reflects the much heavier police presence in Ireland than in England and Wales. The higher rate of arrests for public drunkenness may also be read as a reflection of the fact that there were more police around to arrest drunken persons in Ireland than in England and Wales. W. Neilson Hancock, who prepared the Irish judicial statistics in the 1860s, supports the general point in a significant observation on the judicial statistics for 1868:

> the fact that the Irish police act as inspectors of weights and measures, and as a revenue police, would naturally lead to a greater vigilance in enforcing these Acts, and the much larger proportion of police to population in Ireland than in England and Wales would also lead to greater activity in the detection and punishment of minor offences, especially as the justices have power to award one-third of the pecuniary penalties (the usual punishment for such offences), to the constabulary award fund.

Hancock pointed to the charges against prostitutes as another illustration of the effect that Ireland's relatively higher police presence had on crime returns: while

---

40 V.A.C. Gatrell and T.B. Hadden, 'Criminal statistics and their interpretation' in E.A. Wrigley (ed.), *Nineteenth-century society: essays in the use of quantitative methods for the study of social data* (London, 1972), pp 336–96. Scottish crime was tabulated separately from that of England and Wales.

5 Extract from *Return of judicial statistics of Ireland, 1863* HC 1864 [3418] lvii 653.

there were 2,920 prostitutes known to the Irish police in 1868 (roughly equivalent to 6,570 in an equal proportion of the population of England and Wales), the Irish police brought some 4,393 charges against prostitutes under the Vagrancy Acts, as compared with 1,831 in an equal proportion of the population of England and Wales.[41]

Another factor to take into account when analysing Irish crime statistics is that they were, to an unquantifiable degree, artificially inflated by periodic increases of police activity – at the behest of superior officers – against certain illegal activities. These were usually misdemeanours, including such categories as dog owners in towns and cities failing to muzzle their pets,[42] cyclists riding bicycles on footpaths or farmers allowing their animals to stray on the roads. One should also note that the method of tabulating statistics of non-indictable offences changed in 1895, to bring them more into line with the system used in England and Wales. These changes resulted in a considerable fall in the number of non-indictable offences recorded annually in Ireland, and mean that the Irish statistics of non-indictable offences from 1895 onwards are not directly comparable with those before 1894.

Another problem with the Irish returns is that the statistics of agrarian outrages are not entirely reliable. As W.E. Vaughan has argued, when the constabulary compiled statistical returns of crime 'agrarian outrage was a convenient taxonomical receptacle for all disputes that were remotely connected with land', and some of these were remote indeed.[43] The RIC also introduced significant changes to their method of recording agrarian outrages in 1869, of which the researcher should be aware. The chief secretary for Ireland, Arthur Balfour, explained in May 1887 that the RIC in 1869 and 1870 used a system of enumerating such outrages as levying contributions, administering unlawful oaths and sending threatening letters, which considerably increased their total and prevents an exact comparison being drawn between the outrage statistics for those years and other years. He gave the example of a party of about twenty men who visited thirty houses in County Mayo on 27 December 1869 and had the inhabitants swear 'on a book' that they would not pay more than the government valuation for their land. They also 'levied contributions' at each house. These were recorded as thirty separate cases of administering unlawful oaths and thirty separate cases of levying contributions. However, by the earlier method used by the RIC, this would have been recorded as merely one instance of administering unlawful oaths and one instance of levying contributions, when the acts were committed by the same party. Balfour also gave the example of 22 threatening notices being posted on 13 January 1870 on the houses of 22 people in one townland in County Mayo. These threatened with death any person who paid more than the government valuation for their land. This episode was recorded as

---

41 *Return of judicial statistics of Ireland, 1868* HC 1868–69 [4203] lviii 737, p. 17. For a discussion of Hancock's career see John F. McEldowney, 'William Neilson Hancock (1822–1888)' in *Irish Jurist*, xx (1988), pp 378–402.   **42** Brian Griffin, '"Mad dogs and Irishmen": dogs and rabies in the eighteenth and nineteenth centuries' in *Ulster Folklife*, 40 (1994), pp 1–15.   **43** Vaughan, *Landlords and tenants in mid-Victorian Ireland*, pp 141–49.

twenty-two separate offences, whereas the constabulary would have recorded it as one offence in 1868 or earlier. The new system recorded 82 outrages, whereas the earlier system would have recorded only three. In 1871 the earlier system of recording was reintroduced.[44]

In addition to this anomaly, the RIC sometimes failed to record as agrarian offences crimes that did not meet a strict definition of what constituted an agrarian offence, even though it might seem to the researcher that these crimes were definitely agrarian in nature. As Arthur Balfour explained, after the crime returns produced during W.E. Forster's period as chief secretary[45] came under severe criticism in parliament, 'the natural consequence has been that the authorities in Ireland have been more and more strict in their requirements before they permitted any crime to be classified as agrarian'. According to Balfour:

> in order that a crime may be classed as agrarian, it is not merely necessary that it should arise out of social disorganisation, consequent or possibly consequent upon agrarian discontent, but it must be directly traceable to outrages, [with] some specific motive connected with land, so that a large number of crimes specially characteristic of Irish disorder, such as the maiming of cattle, firing into houses, moonlighting, and raiding for arms, may never appear in the returns at all.

Among examples of well-known crimes that were not returned as agrarian outrages, Balfour referred to the Curtin case of November 1885.[46] In this incident, a number of men called to the house of the Curtins, a farming family who held 160 acres of land near Firies, County Kerry, and demanded arms from them. John Curtin was vice-president of the Firies branch of the National League, and his two sons were members of the organisation. Curtin had, however, paid his rent to his landlord, Lord Kenmare, and was apparently negotiating on behalf of the tenants for an abatement. In the arms raid John Curtin fired on the visiting party and killed one of them, and he in turn was killed by one of the raiders. Why the authorities insisted that this was not an agrarian outrage is not clear.[47]

To complicate the issue still further, incidents that appear as straightforward cases of agrarian crime were sometimes nothing of the sort. For instance, in May 1888, Sergeant Hutchinson of the RIC told the Dungannon presentment sessions that he had recorded an incident of barn-burning in the area as a case of agrarian outrage, even though the evidence suggested that it was an accident and he believed that this was the case. Hutchinson explained that in such unclear cases, incidents were recorded as outrages rather than accidents,[48] which certainly calls into ques-

---

44 *Freeman's Journal*, 24 May 1887; *Memorandum as to the principle upon which outrages are recorded as agrarian, and included as such in the returns laid before parliament* HC 1887 (140) lxviii 25. **45** Forster was chief secretary for Ireland from April 1880 to May 1882. **46** *Freeman's Journal*, 24 May 1887. **47** Details from Margaret O'Callaghan, 'Parnellism and crime: constructing a Conservative strategy of containment 1887–91' in Donal McCartney (ed.), *Parnell: the politics of power* (Dublin, 1991), pp 114–15. **48** *Freeman's*

tion earlier claims that the authorities were being much more rigorous in their definitions of what constituted an agrarian outrage. G. Garrow Green, a constabulary officer in the final quarter of the nineteenth century, claims in his memoirs that 'at least 50 per cent' of supposed outrages, such as threatening letters, cattle-maiming and arson attacks, were 'uncoupled with malice'.[49]

His memoirs, one of a number of useful first-hand accounts by policemen of their experiences in Ireland, are instructive for the light that they throw on supposed agrarian outrages:

> For instance, I have known an estate-owner employ his steward to write him a threatening letter because a police-barrack, his property, for which he received government rent, was about to be given up. Another wrote himself a similar letter and fired a gun-shot at his own window, simply because he wanted to have one or two of our men stationed in his house, whom he used to employ in various ways, and have driving him about as a sort of guard of honour. Two head stewards wrote threatening letters to themselves to enhance their value in their masters' eyes, and have their wages increased. But though now and then such cases crop up, the great proportion arises from greedy endeavours to amass money. This may be done by obtaining compensation under the Malicious Injury to Properties Act, off the barony, which is levied by an order of the justices at a presentment sessions, if satisfied that the applicant has sustained the injury alleged of malice prepense. It is no doubt a great temptation to avaricious and unscrupulous persons to do themselves, say, a £10 injury and mulct their neighbours of five times as much by exaggeration.
>
> In some instances, a hay-rick (or two) is carefully fired, and, when its destruction is only a matter of time – i.e., not counting what has been first abstracted and stowed away elsewhere – a breathless messenger, well-primed with pseudo-innocent information, will knock at the door of the nearest RIC and clamour for assistance.[50]

Green gives another example of a bogus outrage, in which a farmer purchased a second farm, on the lands of which there was a 'substantial dwelling-house' which was uninhabited. This house was burned to the ground shortly after the farmer had received a threatening letter. Instead of being an act of malicious arson, the burning was done by the farmer and his son, with the rest of the farmer's children keeping a look-out while the arsonists went about their task.[51] While Green's testimony shows that the R.I.C were aware that crafty farmers and others were attempting to commit fraud by fabricating agrarian crime, it is inconceivable that the police were aware of all such efforts and that the official crime returns do not include bogus outrages as well as genuine agrarian outrages.

Journal, 21 May 1888. **49** G. Garrow Green, *In the Royal Irish Constabulary* (London, 1905), p. 229. **50** Ibid., pp 231–2. **51** Ibid., pp 232–3.

The researcher, then, needs to be careful when using the crime and outrage statistics in the parliamentary papers. The crime returns are not as comprehensive as one would wish, and the statistics themselves are open to more than one reading. Nevertheless, imperfect as they are, they give the researcher a broad snapshot of the incidence of crime, or at least of crimes known to the police. Contemporaries were aware of their interpretative potential, as evidenced by a number of articles that rely on police returns of crime as their main source of information,[52] and the modern researcher can certainly use such material to provide a general statistical overview of crime at local level, provided that he or she is aware of the methodological problems inherent in the crime and outrage returns.[53]

MEMOIRS, DIARIES, TRAVELLERS' ACCOUNTS

The period from 1801 to 1921 saw the production of numerous memoirs, published diaries and descriptions by travellers of their journeys in Ireland.[54] Judge Fletcher, in his charge to the Wexford grand jury in August 1814, poured scorn on the descriptions of crime and disturbance in many of these travellers' accounts:

> Does a visitor come to Ireland, to compile a book of travels, what is his course? He is handed about from one country gentleman to another, all interested in concealing from him the true state of the country; he passes from squire to squire, each rivalling the other in entertaining their guest – all busy in pouring falsehoods into his ears, touching the disturbed state of the country, and the vicious habits of the people.
>
> Such is the crusade of information, upon which the English traveller sets forward; and he returns to his own country with all his unfortunate prejudices doubled and confirmed – in a kind of moral despair of the welfare of such a wicked race, having made up his mind that nothing ought to be done for this lawless and degraded country.[55]

---

52 James Haughton, *On the connexion between intemperance and crime* (Dublin, 1849); idem, *Statistics of crime* (Dublin, 1850); idem, *Statistics to illustrate the connexion between ignorance and crime* (Dublin, 1852); anonymous author, 'A glance at Irish statistics' in *Dublin University Magazine*, xlv, no. cclxvi (Feb. 1855), pp 243–52; John Moncrieff Wilson, *Statistics of crime in Ireland, 1842 to 1856* (Dublin, 1857); Mark S. O'Shaughnessy, 'On criminal statistics; especially with reference to population, education, and distress in Ireland' in *Journal of the Statistical and Social Inquiry Society of Ireland*, iv, part 23 (Oct. 1864), pp 91–104. **53** James W. Hurst, 'Disturbed Tipperary: 1831–1860' in *Éire-Ireland*, ix, no. 3 (autumn 1974), pp 44–59; David Fitzpatrick, 'The geography of Irish nationalism 1910–1921' in *Past & Present*, no. 78 (1978), pp 113–44; Joseph Lee, 'Patterns of rural unrest in nineteenth-century Ireland: a preliminary survey' in Cullen and Furet (eds), *Ireland and France 17th–20th centuries*, pp 223–37; Andrew W. Orridge, 'Who supported the Land War? An aggregate-data analysis of Irish agrarian discontent, 1879–1882' in *Economic and Social Review*, 12, no. 3 (Apr. 1981), pp 203–33; David Johnson, 'Trial by jury'. **54** For a guide to travellers' published accounts see John McVeagh, *Irish travel writing: a bibliography* (Dublin, 1996). **55** *The charge of Judge Fletcher to the grand jury of the county of Wexford at the summer assizes, on Friday, 5th August, 1814* (Dublin, 1814), pp 14–15.

While the judge's description undoubtedly holds true concerning the *modus operandi* of some foreign travel writers in the country, it would be unwise to discount all such authors' published details of their trips to Ireland and the accounts of crime and disorder that they often contain. On the contrary, such sources frequently offer a contradictory or more sympathetic portrayal of crime and popular disturbances than one would suppose from Judge Fletcher's comments. Travellers' descriptions should certainly be read with an eye to such features as sensationalism or bias; the same applies to reading published diaries and memoirs, and the diarists and memoirists may also have been prone to selective or faulty memory. Nevertheless, these contemporary sources represent an important resource to the researcher on crime in this period.

A particularly valuable memoir for the study of crime in pre-Famine Ireland is that of James Anton, a sergeant in the 42nd Regiment who served from 1814 to 1815 and from 1817 to 1825 in various parts of Leinster and Munster. Anton provides a fascinating outsider's view into the widespread rural disorder that he was involved in trying to suppress during those years, notably the Rockite disturbances in County Limerick. While much of the South of Ireland was undoubtedly disturbed in this period, Anton provides an interesting observation on the tendency of the constabulary to write alarmist accounts of the state of the country, which the researcher reading police reports in the National Archives and other repositories should bear in mind:

> Two constables were attached to our party, relieving each other alternately, once every two weeks, so that only one remained at the barrack: from both we received an exaggerated account of the state of the public feeling around us. One, in particular, was always sounding the tocsin of alarm in our ears. A party of *Whiteboys*, *Shanavites* [sic], *Caravites* [sic], or *Carders*, had been seen in such a direction, several shots had been heard in another; all was verbal report, through a long transmission from one credulous person to another, until it reached the constable, and a report had to be forwarded to the magistrate; in consequence of which a party was ordered out towards the reported place of alarm, on purpose to ascertain the certainty or cause; and after patrolling the country for miles, it returned satisfied that the report was founded in falsehood, and that no cause existed to suspect that the people had been otherwise employed than in their usual domestic or agricultural pursuits.[56]

Other important contemporary military memoirs or diaries include the published journal of Henry McClintock, and the published recollections of George Calladine and Joseph Donaldson. Donaldson, who first arrived in Ireland in 1814 and was stationed in Cork and Mayo for a few years, also provides evidence that the police

---

56 James Anton, *Retrospect of a military life* (Edinburgh, 1845), p. 160. The district referred to is Tullaroan, County Kilkenny.

and magistrates were sometimes prone to exaggerate the level of crime and outrage. Describing his period in Mayo, he states that

> In the course of duty, I was one of a detachment sent to a village about twenty miles from head-quarters, where the inhabitants were in a disturbed state. From the accounts given us by the constables when we first went there, we were led to believe that the whole country was in arms, ready, when the word was given, to massacre all opposed to their schemes. But we soon found that their fears or their prejudices had magnified the cause of alarm to a wonderful degree. Before we became acquainted with the true state of affairs, they made us complete hacks, calling us out to their assistance in every drunken squabble which took place, often through their own insolent behaviour.[57]

After relating the details of one false alarm, when the soldiers were summoned during the night by a panic-stricken (and probably drunk) policeman to disperse a supposed party of Shanavests, which turned out to be a herd of heifers grazing in a field, Donaldon's account continues:

> For some time we were regularly called out by these fellows, when they went to destrain[sic] a man's goods for rent or tythes[sic], until we were more like the bailiff's body guard than any thing else. But after being made fools of in this way two or three times, our officer remonstrated and arranged matters so, that we were not obliged to go out without a special order from the magistrate. This relieved us from the petty affairs more immediately under the cognizance of the constable, but still we had enough to do in following after the magistrate, who seemed to consider a hunt after his countrymen even more amusing than one after the fox. Had the people been peaceably inclined, his conduct would have goaded them on to outrage. He was continually up to his ears in business – some momentous matter always in hand. Every trifling riot was magnified into a deep-laid rebellion – if a cabin or a hay-stack was set on fire, a whole village was consumed – if one man was wounded, a dozen were killed, and so on, always magnifying the event in proportion to the distance.[58]

Calladine, who was stationed in several counties in Leinster, Munster and Connacht between 1821 and 1830, provides an eyewitness account of the troubled state of the areas in which he served, as well as an interesting description of a raid for poteen in Leitrim in the summer of 1823. McClintock, an official in Dundalk Custom House, was also a yeomanry officer. His recently published journal contains numerous references to crime and criminals in Louth in the first two decades of the nineteenth century.[59]

[57] Joseph Donaldson, *Scenes and sketches of a soldier's life in Ireland* (Edinburgh, 1826), p. 94. [58] Ibid., pp 95–97. [59] M.L. Ferrar (ed.), *The diary of Colour-Serjeant George Calladine 19th Foot 1793–1837* (London,

Taken together, these contemporary sources give a level-headed description of crime at the local level from the perspective of some members of the armed forces engaged in aiding the civil power in pre-Famine Ireland. A more alarmist and sensationalist view, from an anonymous Tipperary magistrate, is given in *The present state of Tipperary, as regards agrarian outrages, their nature, origin, and increase, considered, with suggestions for remedial measures* (Dublin, 1842). The details of several agrarian murders in County Tipperary in 1840 and 1841 are discussed in this publication. The sensationalist nature of the text (with the author arguing that many of the outrages discussed 'are so heinous in their nature – so marked by cruelty, atrocity, and barbarity – as to equal, if not exceed in their details, those of the most savage nations of the earth, excepting only the absence of cannibalism') reflects the panic-stricken tone of many of the magistrate reports to Dublin Castle in the pre-Famine period.[60]

Apart from evidence gleaned from those engaged in enforcing or attempting to enforce law and order, the researcher may make use of other contemporary sources that give a glimpse of crime or disorder at local level. The diaries of the schoolteacher, Humphrey O'Sullivan of Callan, County Kilkenny, frequently refer to these subjects.[61] An English tourist's anonymously authored *Excursions from Bandon, in the South of Ireland* (London, 1825) describes the workings of the Clonakilty petty sessions in 1825, while Henry D. Inglis, *A journey throughout Ireland, during the spring, summer, and autumn of 1834* (2 vols, London, 1834) contains fascinating discussions of petty sessions cases at Mitchelstown, Tralee and Westport, as well as an account of the Clare assizes. William Makepeace Thackeray's *The Irish sketchbook, 1842* (London, 1843) provides a similar glimpse of Waterford assizes cases in the summer of 1842.

Three works by foreign commentators in the 1830s are frequently drawn upon by historians studying social conditions in pre-Famine Ireland, and they are also recommended to the researcher into crime in this period. Gustave de Beaumont, *Ireland: social, political and religious* (2 vols, London, 1839) gives a sympathetic account of the numerous outbreaks of agrarian crime before the Famine. Alexis de Tocqueville's account of his travels in Ireland in July and August 1835 contains plenty of detail on crime and disorder, as well as his own and other contemporaries' musings on the causes of the crimes that he describs.[62] George Cornewall Lewis's *On local disturbances in Ireland; and on the Irish Church question* (London, 1836), based largely on a judicious trawl through contemporary publications, remains an indispensable set of descriptions and interpretations of Irish crime in the 1820s and 1830s.

1922); Pádraig Ó Néill (ed.), *Journal of Henry McClintock* (Dundalk, 2001). For a discussion of the role of the yeomanry in aid of the civil power see Allan Blackstock, *An ascendancy army: the Irish yeomanry, 1796–1834* (Dublin, 1998), pp 232–68. **60** Stanley H. Palmer, *Police and crime in England and Ireland, 1780–1850* (Cambridge, 1988), pp 198, 199–200. **61** Michael McGrath (ed.), *Cinnlae Amhlaoibh Uí Shuileabháin. The diary of Humphrey O'Sullivan Part I containing the diary from 1st January, 1827 to the end of August, 1828* (Dublin, 1936); *Part II containing the diary from 1st September 1828 to the end of December, 1830* (Dublin, 1936); *Part III containing the diary from 1st January, 1831 to the end of December, 1833* (Dublin, 1936). **62** Emmet Larkin (ed.), *Alexis de Tocqueville's journey in Ireland July–August, 1835* (Washington, D.C., 1990).

Although the Famine precipitated the publication of numerous visitors' descriptions of their travels in Ireland, few of these allude directly to crime or disturbance.[63] They may still be read with profit by the historian of crime in this period, however, as they throw light on the level of distress in various parts of the country which often pushed the desperate into committing illegal acts.[64] One of the few contemporary works to discuss crime during the Famine is Asenath Nicholson's *Annals of the Famine in Ireland, in 1847, 1848 and 1849* (New York, 1851), although most of the book focuses on the scenes of destitution and hunger that Nicholson witnessed.[65] Another important source, although one that must be used with caution, is W. Steuart Trench's account of his work as a land agent for the marquis of Lansdowne and marquis of Bath in Kerry, Tipperary and Monaghan in the 1840s and 1850s. His memoirs describe agrarian murders and other agrarian outrages in Tipperary in the early 1840s, and also contain a description of popular resistance to the serving of processes in Farney, County Monaghan, including the 'Battle of Magheracloone'. This is the name given to the affray in which a party of constabulary, who were protecting a bailiff posting notices about the serving of processes on the Catholic church wall, were attacked by a stone-throwing mob. The constabulary opened fire on the mob, killing one person and wounding five. The memoirs also contain a fanciful account of the 'Ribbon Confederacy' on Lord Bath's Monaghan estate, including a lengthy description – supposedly based on an informer's evidence – of a 'Ribbon trial' of Trench, in which Trench was sentenced to death.[66] Matilda Charlotte Houstoun's *Twenty years in the wild west; or Life in Connaught* (London, 1879) gives an anecdotal but not unworthwhile view of life in Mayo, including an account of agrarian crime there. Houstoun's memoir is coloured by a hostility to the Mayo tenantry (whom she refers to as 'aborigines') and the Catholic clergy, as suggested by the following description of the 'cotters' of her neighbourhood:

> Lawless, predatory specimens of the human race were they; men, women and children, whose civilisation had never even been attempted. More dan-

---

63 For secondary sources that discuss crime at the local level during the Famine see Andrés Eiríksson, 'Food supply and riots' in Cormac Ó Gráda (ed.), *Famine 150: commemorative lecture series* (Dublin, 1997), pp 67–93; William Fraher, 'The Dungarvan disturbances of 1846 and sequels' in Des Cowman and Donald Brady (eds), *The Famine in Waterford, 1845–1850: teacht na bprátaí dubha* (Dublin, 1995), pp 137–52; Anne Coleman, *Riotous Roscommon: social unrest in the 1840s* (Dublin, 1999). For general discussions see W.J. Lowe, 'Policing Famine Ireland' in *Éire-Ireland*, xxix, no. 4 (winter 1994), pp 47–67 and Christine Kinealy, *The Great Irish Famine: impact, ideology and rebellion* (New York and Basingstoke, 2002), pp 117–48. **64** For the immediate pre-Famine period see A.M. and S.C. Hall, *Ireland: its scenery, character &c* (3 vols, London, 1841–43); J.G. Kohl, *Travels in Ireland* (London, 1844); James Johnson, *A tour in Ireland* (London, 1844); Asenath Nicholson, *Ireland's welcome to the stranger: or, excursions through Ireland in 1844 and 1845 for the purpose of personally investigating the condition of the poor* (London, 1847). For the Great Famine years see Alexander Somerville, *Letters from Ireland during the Famine of 1847* ed. K.D.M. Snell (Dublin, 1998) and John Killen (ed.), *The Famine decade: contemporary accounts, 1841–1851* (Belfast, 1995). **65** A new edition, edited by Maureen Murphy, has been published by Lilliput Press with the shortened title of *Annals of the Famine in Ireland* (Dublin, 1998). **66** W. Steuart Trench, *Realities of Irish life* (London, 1868).

The hands were shut close and tight, and were exactly in the attitude of a man sparring desperately with his adversary.

6 Extract from W. Steuart Trench, *Realities of Irish life* (London, 1868).

gerous neighbours were they by far than the warlike Zulus, inasmuch as the 'strong back' on which they leant, was that body of human beings professing Christianity, and arrogating to themselves the right to remit sins.[67]

Hugh Dorian's memoirs, which describe life in the Fánaid peninsula in Donegal during the Famine years and the decade after it, contain a lot of detail about illicit distillation and poteen smuggling and the attempts of the Revenue Police (abolished in 1857) and the Irish Constabulary to suppress this illegal activity.[68] A source that describes life in Belfast around the same period is the Reverend William Murphy O'Hanlon's *Walks among the poor of Belfast* (Belfast and Dublin, 1853). While the clergyman's main concern in publishing this book was to expose the appalling living conditions endured by the poor in Belfast's slums during the 1850s, his powerful indictment also provides details of prostitution and crime in these districts. His book is one of the few contemporary published sources for the study of urban crime in nineteenth-century Ireland.[69] Julius Rodenberg's *A pilgrimage through Ireland, or*

---

[67] Matilda Charlotte Houstoun, *Twenty years in the wild west; or Life in Connaught* (London, 1879), p. 228. [68] Hugh Dorian, *The outer edge of Ulster: a memoir of social life in nineteenth-century Donegal*, ed. Breandán Mac Suibhne and David Dickson (Notre Dame, 2000), pp 272–300. [69] For more details on crime in Belfast in this period see Brian Griffin, *The Bulkies: police and crime in Belfast, 1800–1865*

the island of the saints (London, 1860) contains details of the author's visit to Belfast in 1859 which may be used in conjunction with *Walks among the poor of Belfast*, as it also discusses the problem of crime and prostitution in various parts of the city. The anonymously published *The wren of the Curragh* (London, 1867) is a colourful and not unsympathetic portrayal of the Curragh 'wrens', the 50 to 60 prostitutes who lived in wretched conditions near the Curragh military camp in the 1860s.[70] The historian researching crime in Dublin may turn to Frank Thorpe Porter, *Twenty years' recollections of an Irish police magistrate* (Dublin, 1889, 8th edition) for an anecdotal account of crime in the capital city during the author's time as a police magistrate, from the 1840s to the 1860s.

Most published accounts of illegal activity in the 1860s focus on Fenianism. One of the few that does not is Sir Henry John Brownrigg, *Examination of some recent allegations concerning the constabulary force in Ireland, in a report to his excellency the lord lieutenant* (Dublin, 1864). Brownrigg, the inspector general of the Irish Constabulary, felt compelled to produce this publication in order to refute what he saw as the unfounded claims by numerous magistrates, judges, grand juries and newspaper editors that the police were unsuited to the work of preventing or detecting agrarian crime, which was perceived to be undergoing an alarming increase in many counties at the time. Brownrigg's book provides detailed descriptions of crime, particularly agrarian crime, in several counties in the early 1860s, and draws upon correspondence to the under secretary for Ireland, crown solicitors and to himself from chairmen of quarter sessions and county inspectors of constabulary, as well as extracts from contemporary newspapers, to present a more favourable picture of the state of crime. Lengthy extracts from judges' favourable charges to county grand juries form a large part of Brownrigg's book, as do extracts from county inspectors' reports on the level of crime in their counties. The county inspector for Cavan expressed an interesting, cynical view of some of the more serious apparent crimes in his county:

> As to incendiary fires, every burning in this county, with very few exceptions, is called malicious – even when it is generally believed it had its origins in the carelessness of the people themselves; and when the Police hear of such burnings, and make inquiry, they receive very little assistance from the owners, as there is an opinion amongst the country people that, in case of a detection, there can be no claim for damages off the county.

(Dublin, 1997), pp 59–88. For a discussion of crime in Dublin in the late nineteenth and early twentieth centuries see Joseph V. O'Brien, *'Dear, dirty Dublin': a city in distress, 1899–1916* (Berkeley and Los Angeles, 1982), pp 179–98. **70** I would like to thank Maria Luddy for this reference. For a closer look at prostitution in nineteenth-century Ireland see Dr Luddy's three articles, 'Prostitution and rescue work in nineteenth-century Ireland' in Maria Luddy and Cliona Murphy (eds), *Women surviving: studies in Irish women's history in the nineteenth and twentieth centuries* (Swords, 1989), pp 51–84; 'An outcast community: the "wrens" of the Curragh' in *Women's History Review*, 1, no. 3 (1992), pp 341–55; 'Abandoned women and bad characters: prostitution in nineteenth-century Ireland' in *Women's History Review*, 6, no. 4 (1997), pp 485–503.

The county inspector for Roscommon reported a similar state of affairs regarding some house burnings in his county.[71] Given the type and detailed nature of the sources used by Brownrigg, his book is indispensable for the student of crime in Ireland, especially agrarian crime, in the late 1850s and early 1860s.[72]

Much of Brownrigg's time in this period was taken up with trying to combat the activities of the Fenian organisation.[73] Despite the fact that it was a secret society – but fortunately for the historian – many Fenians published their memoirs. These are invaluable for the researcher trying to piece together the activities of the organisation at the local level.[74] Jeremiah O'Donovan Rossa, *Rossa's recollections* (Mariner's Harbor, New York, 1898) is useful for studying the early history of the Fenian movement in West Cork. John Devoy, *Recollections of an Irish rebel* (New York, 1929) gives plenty of information about the leading Fenian personalities and Fenian activities at local level, although one should treat some of his statistics – such as his claim that there were 'fully 1,500' members of the organisation in the district of Stratford, County Wicklow, in 1864 – with caution. Devoy has disappointingly little to say about the Fenian movement in Ulster, but the researcher can turn instead to the memoirs of James Mullin for an account of the organisation in Cookstown,[75] while Frank Roney's autobiography is invaluable for the historian researching

---

[71] Henry John Brownrigg, *Examination of some recent allegations concerning the constabulary force in Ireland, in a report to his excellency the lord lieutenant* (Dublin, 1864), pp 63, 65. [72] For the economic background to the agrarian crime of this period see James S. Donnelly, jr, 'The Irish agricultural depression of 1859–64' in *Irish Economic and Social History*, ii (1976), pp 33–54. Three secondary sources that examine localised instances of agrarian crime in the 1850s and 1860s are Liam Dolan, *Land war and eviction in Derryveagh, 1840–65* (Dundalk, 1980); W.E. Vaughan, *Sin, sheep and Scotsmen: John George Adair and the Derryveagh evictions* (Belfast, 1983); Homer E. Socolofsky, *Landlord William Scully* (Lawrence, 1979). [73] For a bibliographical survey see Patrick J. Quinlivan, 'Hunting the Fenians: problems in the historiography of a secret organisation' in Patrick O'Sullivan (ed.), *The Irish world wide: history, heritage, identity. Volume 3: the creative migrant* (Leicester, 1994), pp 133–53. [74] The best general starting points in the secondary literature are T.W. Moody (ed.), *The Fenian movement* (Cork, 1968); Comerford, 'Patriotism as pastime'; idem, *Fenians in context*. For studies of Fenianism at the local level before the 1867 rebellion see the following: Charles Rice, 'Fenianism in Monaghan' in *Clogher Record*, i, no. 4 (1956), pp 29–84; Brian Mac Cafaid, 'Fenianism and Co. Donegal' in *Donegal Annual*, vii, no. 2 (1967), pp 135–47; Breandán Mac Giolla Choille, 'Fenians, Rice, and Ribbonism in County Monaghan, 1864–67' in *Clogher Record*, vi, no. 2 (1967), pp 221–52; Seán Ó Lúing, 'A contribution to the study of Fenianism in Breifne' in *Breifne*, iii, no. 10 (1967), pp 155–74; Pádraig G. Ó Laighin, *Fíníní Laoise* (Dublin, 1990). For local studies of the rebellion see W. McGrath, 'The Fenian rising in Cork' in *Irish Sword*, viii, no. 33 (1968), pp 322–35; Shin-ichi Takagami, 'The Fenian rising in Dublin, March 1867' in *Irish Historical Studies*, xxix, no. 115 (May 1995), pp 340–62; Seán Ó Lúing, 'Aspects of the Fenian rising in Kerry, 1867. I. The rising and its background' in *Journal of the Kerry Archaeological and Historical Society*, no. 3 (1970), pp 131–53; idem, 'Aspects of the Fenian rising in Kerry, 1867. II. Aftermath' in *Journal of the Kerry Archaeological and Historical Society*, no. 4 (1971), pp 139–64; idem, 'Aspects of the Fenian rising in Kerry, 1867. III. Prelude to the trials' in *Journal of the Kerry Archaeological and Historical Society*, no. 5 (1972), pp 103–32; idem, 'Aspects of the Fenian rising in Kerry, 1867. IV. Kerry summer assizes, 1867' in *Journal of the Kerry Archaeological and Historical Society*, no. 6 (1973), pp 172–94; idem, 'Aspects of the Fenian rising in Kerry, 1867. V. Personalities and problems' in *Journal of the Kerry Archaeological and Historical Society*, no. 7 (1974), pp 107–33. For a local study of the organisation after the rising see Shin-ichi Takagami, *The Dublin Fenians after the rising, 1867–79* (Tokyo, 1992). [75] James Mullin, *The story of a toiler's life*, ed. Patrick Maume (Dublin, 2000).

Fenianism in Belfast and its vicinity.[76] Joseph Denieffe, *A personal narrative of the Irish Revolutionary Brotherhood* (New York, 1906) contains useful details about the personnel and activity of the organisation in the rest of the country. John O'Leary, *Recollections of Fenians and Fenianism* (2 vols, London, 1896) also deals with Fenianism throughout Ireland. Much of this book regurgitates details supplied to the author by Thomas Clarke Luby in a lengthy correspondence. The latter unsurpassable material, enlivened by Luby's engaging and inimitable sense of humour, is available in the National Library's manuscript department.[77]

The Land War was the catalyst for numerous publications by contemporary observers. Researchers should be aware that these tend to fall into two main categories: accounts that are sympathetic to the Land League or National League, and others that tend to be sympathetic to landlords and the Dublin Castle authorities who were attempting to curb the activities of agrarian agitators and their supporters. Although many of the former do not explicitly support or condone the agrarian violence and disturbances of the period, they do tend to explain agrarian outrages in terms of their being the actions of a desperate peasantry driven to violent extremes by rackrenting landlords. Michael Davitt's *The fall of feudalism in Ireland or the story of the Land League revolution* (London and New York, 1904), is the classic example of this approach, and this may be supplemented by Dana Hearne's edition of Anna Parnell's *The tale of a great sham* (Dublin, 1986).[78] Publications that tend to view the landlords and the Dublin Castle administration in a hostile light include G. Shaw Léfèvre, *Incidents of coercion: a journal of visits to Ireland in 1882 and 1888* (London, 1889) and *Combination and coercion* (London, 1890), J.L. Joynes, *The adventures of a tourist in Ireland* (London, 1882), John Curry, *The Barbavilla trials and the Crimes Act in Ireland* (Dublin, 1885)[79] Paschal Grousset, *Ireland's disease: the English in Ireland, 1887* (London, 1888), 'Zeno', *Ireland in '89* (Providence, 1889) and Fr Thomas Conefry, *A short history of the land war in Drumlish in 1881* (Dublin, 1892).

George Pellew, *In castle and cabin or talks in Ireland in 1887* (New York and London, 1888) is an important contemporary source as it gives a comparatively even-handed account of the Land War. Pellew, a member of the Suffolk bar, travelled widely throughout Ireland in 1887 and interviewed such people as boycotted farmers in Cork, members of the National League, magistrates, priests and landlords on Plan of Campaign estates in Cork, Waterford and Galway, as well as describing evictions that he witnessed at Gweedore, County Donegal.[80] William Henry Hurlbert also travelled widely throughout the country a year later and interviewed a wide

---

76 Ira B. Cross (ed.), *Frank Roney, Irish rebel and California labor leader* (Berkeley, 1931). See also Seán Ó Lúing, *Ó Donnabháin Rosa I* (Dublin, 1969), pp 179–190 and Catherine Hirst, *Religion, politics and violence in nineteenth-century Belfast: the Pound and Sandy Row* (Dublin, 2002), pp 94–103 for discussions of the IRB in Belfast. **77** MSS 331–333. **78** For a wider discussion of women's role in the Land War see Janet K. TeBrake, 'Irish peasant women in revolt: the Land League years' in *Irish Historical Studies*, xxviii, no. 109 (May 1992), pp 63–80. **79** For a detailed discussion of the Barbavilla murder see Ann Murtagh, *Portrait of a Westmeath tenant community, 1879–85: the Barbavilla murder* (Dublin, 1999). **80** See also Wilfrid Scawen Blunt, *The Land War in Ireland* (London, 1912).

range of people, as Pellew did, but produced a much more hostile picture of the National League and its sympathisers in *Ireland under coercion: the diary of an American* (2 vols, Edinburgh, 1888). Samuel Hussey, *Reminiscences of an Irish land agent* (London, 1904) not surprisingly presents a view of the Land War that is extremely hostile to the supporters of the land agitation. It is particularly detailed on events in Kerry in the 1880s. The anonymously authored *Irish agitation* (Dublin, 1880) is a work of anti-Land League propaganda that records extracts from seditious speeches at Land League meetings. It also contains extracts from speeches by Catholic clergymen and other public figures condemning the Land League, and brief details of agrarian outrages throughout Ireland in November and December 1880.

Several barristers and members of the judiciary and the forces of law and order produced memoirs which refer, at least in part, to their experiences during the Land War. These are often anecdotal and sometimes self-serving, but they are not without worth and may be used by the researcher to throw light on specific incidents during this period. Matthias McDonnell Bodkin, *Recollections of an Irish judge: press, bar and parliament* (London, 1914) includes the author's version of his defence of several clients during the Plan of Campaign. John Adye Curran, *Reminiscences of John Adye Curran K.C., late county court judge and chairman of quarter sessions* (London, 1914) details Curran's work as a Dublin divisional magistrate in the early 1880s, especially his role in investigating the Phoenix Park murders, as well as recounting his memories of his time as county court judge in Kerry from 1886 to 1891 and judge and chairman of quarter sessions in Meath, Westmeath, Longford and King's County from 1891 to 1914. The memoirs of Lord O'Brien[81] (better known to nationalists as 'Peter the Packer'), must be treated with caution, not only because they were apparently written by the author with a view to justifying his conduct during the 1880s but also because they were edited after his death by his daughter. O'Brien was variously senior crown solicitor, attorney general and solicitor general for Ireland in the 1880s, and was involved in prosecuting such controversial cases as the murders in Maamtrasna, County Mayo, of five members of the Joyce family,[82] the Invincible trials[83] and the District Inspector Martin murder case in Gweedore in 1889.

There are a number of memoirs by police and others involved in enforcing law and order at this period that are valuable for the insights they give into agrarian dis-

---

81 Georgina O'Brien (ed.), *The reminiscences of the right hon. Lord O'Brien (of Kilfenora), lord chief justice of Ireland* (London, 1916). For a later period, Maurice Healy's *The old Munster circuit* (London, 1939) consists of the author's recollections of cases at various assizes in Munster from 1910 to the outbreak of World War I. **82** For a detailed investigation of the Maamtrasna murders see Jarlath Waldron, *Maamtrasna: the murders and the mystery* (Dublin, 1992). **83** For an admiring account of the Invincibles see P.J.P. Tynan, *The Irish National Invincibles and their times: three decades of struggle against the foreign conspirators in Dublin Castle* (New York, 1894). A different perspective is provided by Tighe Hopkins, *Kilmainham memories: the story of the greatest political crime of the century* (London, 1896). More scholarly discussions are provided by Tom Corfe, *The Phoenix Park murders: conflict, compromise and tragedy in Ireland, 1879–1882* (London, 1968) and Leon Ó Broin, 'The Invincibles' in Williams (ed.), *Secret societies*, pp 113–25.

turbances and other instances of crime in the late nineteenth and early twentieth centuries. Two of the leading figures in the fight against the Land League and National League, respectively, were Charles Dalton Clifford Lloyd and Alfred E. Turner. Clifford Lloyd was a resident magistrate in Belfast, Longford, Limerick and Cork, before being appointed to the post of special resident magistrate (later designated divisional magistrate) in Limerick and Clare in December 1881. Galway was added to his sphere of responsibility in July 1882. Turner, who was a major in the British army in 1882, went to Ireland in that year as assistant to Colonel Sir Henry Brackenburg, who had been appointed to the newly created post of Under-secretary of State for Police and Crime in Ireland. In 1886 Turner was given charge of policing Kerry and Clare, and counties Cork and Limerick were added to his sphere of responsibility in 1889. Their memoirs provide a valuable insight into both law enforcement measures in the 1880s and agrarian crime, although one has to beware of the inherent bias in their accounts, particularly Clifford Lloyd's.[84] Clifford Lloyd's memoirs may be used in conjunction with those of C.P. Crane, who served in the RIC from 1879 to 1897, and as a resident magistrate after finishing his service in the RIC. His autobiography, *Memories of a resident magistrate* (Edinburgh, 1938) is a valuable source for the history of the Land War in Munster, especially Kerry, where Crane served as a district inspector in the early 1880s, and in Donegal, where he served as a district inspector from 1887. A memoir by another constabulary officer, G. Garrow Green, provides a valuable eyewitness account of the Land War, especially in Crossmolina and Tubbercurry, County Mayo and County Sligo, respectively. Although the tone is often whimsical – Killorglin, County Kerry, for example, is referred to as Ballyleatherhead, because of its unruly inhabitants – the memoir is worth persevering with for the insights that it gives into the state of crime and popular sympathy with the perpetrators of agrarian crime. Here is Green's account of the attitude shown in the Tubbercurry region towards a 'returned Yank', Thomas Hunt, who was suspected of murdering a grazier at Buninadden and for whom the RIC searched unsuccessfully:

> It was impossible to avoid noticing the secret, though unexpressed, jubilation of the peasantry at our unprofitable quests. Ireland is indeed a strange country and even Sherlock Holmes would have there no *métier*. Anyone unaccustomed to its eccentricities would suppose that when so unprovoked and barbarous a crime had been committed in their midst, the people would endeavour to wipe out the crimson stain and retrieve the [good] name of the locality by giving the information they certainly could have done if disposed.....On the contrary and without feeling any personal sympathy, they felt their honour was concerned in affording shelter and help of every sort to the ruffian, and the news which sent us on many a wild-goose-chase was artfully contrived to keep Hunt beyond our reach.[85]

84 Clifford Lloyd, *Ireland under the Land League*; Sir Alfred E. Turner, *Sixty years of a soldier's life* (London, 1912). **85** Green, *In the RIC*, p. 105.

Hunt evaded the police and managed to escape to America.

Another useful contemporary source for the study of crime during the Land War years are the published proceedings held under the Special Commission Act of 1888. The special commission was appointed by parliament to inquire into a series of allegations by the London *Times* against most members of the Irish Parliamentary Party and other leading, named participants in the land agitation. These charges amounted to an accusation of being part of a conspiracy whose long-term objective was to win complete independence for Ireland, and whose median-term aim was to bring about the downfall of landlordism in the country, through an illegal campaign of boycotting, intimidation and agrarian outrages, including murder. The attorney general, Sir Richard Webster, led the case for the *Times*, with extraordinary support from Dublin Castle officials: Dublin Castle arranged for district inspectors, resident magistrates and rank-and-file policemen to travel to London to give damning evidence against the Land League and National League and a resident magistrate, W.H. Joyce, was given the task of selecting incriminating documents and witnesses, including victims of agrarian outrages. The special commission sat for 129 sittings between 17 September 1888 and 22 November 1889,[86] and produced the twelve-volume *Special Commission Act, 1888. Reprint of the shorthand notes of the speeches, proceedings, and evidence taken before the commissioners appointed under the above-named Act* (London, 1890). This is a valuable source for the study of the Land War. Not only does it consist of the testimony of eyewitnesses from all walks of Irish life, but it also includes statistical tables of the number and type of agrarian outrages reported in each county from 1877 to 1887 inclusive, and an additional tabular listing of all agrarian crimes in Galway, Mayo, Clare, Kerry and Cork in these years. This gives details of the date and type of offence, the townland in which the offence was committed, the name and other details of the injured person in each instance, and a brief summary by the police of each case.

The troubled events of the early decades of the twentieth century have, like the Land War, produced many contemporary memoirs and other first-hand accounts that the researcher may draw upon. As with the material relating to the Land War, much of this early twentieth-century evidence is highly biased, self-serving or polemical in nature, a fact which the researcher should bear in mind when using it. It nevertheless offers an important additional resource to the parliamentary papers, unpublished manuscripts, newspapers and other contemporary evidence discussed elsewhere in this guide.

The activities of illegal or subversive separatist organisations will probably be of most interest to the researcher in this period, and fortunately many members of these organisations have left published evidence of their actions, as have policemen and other contemporaries. Although women constituted a minority of the formal

---

86 For the special commission see T.W. Moody, '*The Times* versus Parnell, 1887–90' in T.W. Moody (ed.), *Historical studies* (London, 1968), pp 147–82; Ó Broin, *Prime informer*; F.S.L. Lyons, 'Parnellism and crime, 1887–1890' in *Transactions of the Royal Historical Society*, fifth series, 24 (1974), pp 123–40; O'Callaghan, 'Parnellism and crime'.

separatist movement, enough activists in such organisations as Inghinidhe na hÉireann and Cumann na mBan wrote memoirs to allow the researcher to build up a reasonably complete picture of their activities at local level. An essential starting point is Margaret Ward, *In their own voice: women and Irish nationalism* (Dublin, 1995). As well as containing extracts from a range of Republican women's memoirs, this also includes numerous propaganda items from various newspapers and pamphlets.[87] Kathleen Keyes McDonnell, a member of the Gaelic League and Cumann na mBan from Castlelack, County Cork, has recorded her memories of events both before and after the Easter Rising in the Bandon district in *There is a bridge at Bandon: a personal account of the War of Independence* (Cork and Dublin, 1972). Siobhán Lankford was a Gaelic League member who, because of her employment in the Post Office, could not join Cumann na mBan for fear of losing her job. She carried out intelligence work for the IRA during the War of Independence in the Mallow district, and has recorded her recollections of this period in *The hope and the sadness: personal recollections of troubled times in Ireland* (Cork, 1980). Most women memoirists focus on events in Dublin. An episodic perspective on separatist activities in the capital city down to 1914 is provided by the *Sinn Féin* and *Bean na hÉireann* journalist, Sidney Gifford Czira, in *The years flew by* (Dublin, 1974). Two particularly useful memoirs are by women who participated in the Easter rebellion: Máire nic Shiúbhlaigh's *The splendid years* (Dublin, 1955) and Margaret Skinnider, *Doing my bit for Ireland* (New York, 1917). Maud Gonne MacBride's autobiography also has a strong Dublin focus, as has Kathleen Clarke's.[88]

Given that the separatist movement was heavily male dominated, it should come as no surprise that most memoirs and published diaries that give an insider's view of the movement were written by men. Developments in Dublin before and during the Easter Rising are described in Frank Robbins, *Under the starry plough: recollections of the Irish Citizen Army* (Dublin, 1977), Kenneth Griffith and Timothy E. O'Grady (eds), *Curious journey: an oral history of Ireland's unfinished revolution* (London, 1982), Roger McHugh (ed.), *Dublin 1916* (London, 1966) and W.J. Brennan-Whitmore, *Dublin burning: the Easter Rising from behind the barricades* (Dublin, 1996). The narratives that they give of the Rising may be supplemented by other contemporary accounts by non-participants. The *Sinn Fein rebellion handbook*, compiled by the *Weekly Irish Times*, is a voluminous overview of the Rising and its aftermath, whose numerous maps and photographs should prove invaluable to the researcher. James Stephens, *The insurrection in Dublin* (Dublin and London, 1916), Mary Louisa Hamilton Norway, *The Sinn Fein Rebellion as I saw it* (London, 1916) and Adrian and Sally Warwick-Haller (eds), *Letters from Dublin, Easter 1916: Alfred Fannin's diary of the Rising* (Dublin, 1995) are evocative accounts of the events of Easter Week. James Hewitt (ed.), *Eyewitness accounts to Ireland in revolt* (Reading, 1974) also contains a selection of useful first-hand evidence.

---

87 There are a number of brief personal accounts in Maria Luddy (ed.), *Women in Ireland, 1800–1918: a documentary history* (Cork, 1995). **88** There is a full account of women's role in the Easter rising in Ruth Taillon, *When history was made: the women of 1916* (Belfast, 1996).

Numerous recollections have been published by participants in the War of Independence. The classic accounts are Dan Breen, *My fight for Irish freedom* (Dublin, 1924), Ernie O'Malley, *On another man's wound* (Dublin, 1936)[89] and Tom Barry, *Guerilla days in Ireland* (Dublin, 1949). These pay close attention to military activity by the IRA but some of the details need to treated with caution, as Peter Hart has suggested with his forensic examination of Tom Barry's account of the Kilmichael ambush.[90] The *Kerryman* newspaper published compilations of veterans' recollections of their IRA activity in the 1940s. Although these are very one-sided in their tone and perspective, they are still useful to the local historian. The relevant volumes are *Rebel Cork's fighting story, 1916–1921: told by the men who made it* (Tralee, 1947), *Dublin's fighting story, 1913–1921: told by the men who made it* (Tralee, 1947) *Kerry's fighting story, 1916–21: told by the men who made it* (Tralee, 1948) and *Limerick's fighting story 1916–21: told by the men who made it* (Tralee, 1948).[91] Uinseann Mac Eoin, *Survivors* (Dublin, 1980) consists of the recollections of some twenty-three male and female activists in the War of Independence.

Lesser-known veterans' published reminiscences that are valuable for studying the IRA's military and other activity in various areas in this period include Charles Dalton, *With the Dublin Brigade (1917–1921)* (London, 1929); Michael Brennan's *The war in Clare, 1911–1921: personal memoirs of the Irish War of Independence* (Dublin, 1980), an essential source for the student of events in Clare and Limerick; James J. Comerford, *My Kilkenny IRA days, 1916–1922* (Kilkenny, 1978); C.S. Andrews, *Dublin made me: an autobiography* (Dublin and Cork, 1979); Mossie Harnett, *Victory and Woe: the West Limerick Brigade in the War of Independence* (ed.), James H. Joy (Dublin, 2002);[92] Séamas Ó Maoileon, *B'fhiú an braon fola...* (Dublin, 1972), which provides details of the anti-grazier campaign in the Tyrellspass region before World War I, as well as an account of the author's involvement in the IRA's campaign in West Limerick during the War of Independence; Timothy G. McMahon (ed.), *Pádraig Ó Fathaigh's War of Independence: recollections of a Galway Gaelic Leaguer* (Cork, 2000), which describes the activity of the Gort Brigade's intelligence officer in Galway and Clare; and Jeremiah Murphy, *When youth was mine: a memoir of Kerry, 1902–1925* (Dublin, 1998).

A number of policemen's accounts of the early twentieth- century period, including the War of Independence years, are also available to the researcher. Vere T.R. Gregory, *The house of Gregory* (Dublin, 1943) – the memoirs of a man who joined the RIC in 1894 and eventually rose to the rank of county inspector – is interesting on the relatively peaceful state of Ireland for much of the first two decades of the twentieth century. Christopher Lynch-Robinson, *The last of the Irish RMs* (London, 1951) records the experiences of a man who was appointed a resident magistrate in County Donegal in May 1912, before transfer to County Louth, in which latter county he served throughout the War of Independence. Again, much

---

89 See also O'Malley's *Raids and rallies* (Dublin, 1982). **90** Hart, *IRA and its enemies*, pp 22–38. **91** Despite what the subtitles of these books might suggest, the recollections of women activists are also included. **92** I would like to thank my colleague, John Newsinger, for bringing this source to my attention.

of the focus is on the relative tranquillity of society or the non-political nature of the offences with which the author had to deal, although he also includes details of the unsavoury activity of the Black and Tans in Louth and Meath in the period. John D. Brewer, *The Royal Irish Constabulary: an oral history* (Belfast, 1990) consists of the recollections of some fifteen ex-RIC members from the early decades of the twentieth century. Their testimony, which describes their service in numerous Irish counties both before and after the outbreak of World War I, reinforces the impression of a comparative absence of serious crime for much of the period. The RIC men also provide a useful alternative view of IRA activities from the Republican sources discussed earlier in this chapter.[93] Two policemen who eventually changed allegiance and worked for the separatist cause have also produced useful memoirs. Jeremiah Mee served in several stations in County Sligo from February 1911 to July 1919, and in Listowel, County Kerry from July 1919 to June 1920, before resigning in the Listowel mutiny and working in Countess Markiewicz's bureau for ex-policemen. His memoirs provide descriptions of the sort of non-political offences with which the RIC had to deal before the War of Independence, incorporating an amusing account of an unsuccessful hunt for poteen on Inishmurray in June 1918, as well as a valuable description of the War of Independence in Kerry, including the controversial events that led up to the Listowel mutiny.[94] David Neligan, *The spy in the castle* (London, 1963) is the autobiography of a DMP constable who did intelligence work for Michael Collins, and should be of interest to the historian researching the War of Independence in Dublin. For contemporary accounts of the intelligence war from a British perspective see Peter Hart (ed.), *British intelligence in Ireland, 1920–21: the final reports* (Cork, 2002) and Michael Hopkinson (ed.), *The last days of Dublin Castle: the diaries of Mark Sturgis* (Dublin, 1999).

PUBLISHED PROCEEDINGS OF TRIALS

The nineteenth century saw a proliferation of published accounts of proceedings at criminal trials, usually based on the shorthand notes of barristers who were present at the proceedings. These range in size from short pamphlets to quite voluminous publications. Some, such as William G. Chamney, *Report of the trial of the queen a. Thomas Beckham, before the right honorable Mr Justice Fitzgerald, and the right honorable Baron Deasy, at the special commission for the Co. Limerick* (Dublin, 1862) detail the evidence in isolated or unusual cases, such as, in this instance, the trial of Thomas Beckham for murdering Francis Fitzgerald, while attempting to rob him on the road near Kilmallock Hill on 16 May 1862. Most, however, deal with cases which were not just isolated instances of crime that were of little interest outside the immediate locality in which they occurred, but cases that were manifestations of a more general pattern of crime or disturbance. They often relate the proceedings of spe-

---

93 See also the reminiscences of an RIC man's son: Patrick Shea, *Voices and the sound of drums* (Belfast, 1981). **94** J. Anthony Gaughan (ed.), *Memoirs of Constable Jeremiah Mee, RIC* (Dublin, 1975).

cial commissions, court sessions that were instituted when the ordinary quarter sessions or assizes were unable to cope with the volume of cases before them. These publications are useful to the local historian as they provide lengthy and often verbatim accounts of evidence offered at criminal trials, which can be used in conjunction with other contemporary sources to build up a picture of crime or public disorder in local areas.

An early example is William Ridgeway, *A report of the proceedings under a special commission, of oyer and terminer, and gaol delivery, for the counties of Sligo, Mayo, Leitrim, Longford and Cavan, in the month of December, 1806* (Dublin, 1807). Most of the cases tried in these counties were 'Thresher' cases or, in the case of Sligo, 'Thresher' and 'Shaker' cases – the *noms de guerre* of 'John the Thresher' or 'William the Shaker' were variously used when parties visited houses and demanded money or arms in that county. Illegal assembly, demanding arms or money, and taking the Thresher oath were the most common offences dealt with, although there was also one case of conspiracy to murder. James McPhadeen, an old man who was compelled to take the Thresher oath by unnamed men, offered interesting evidence of the Thresher aims in his trial. He was forced by the conspirators to demand of the parish priest of Minola during Mass 'That he should marry persons for half a guinea, baptize for nineteen pence halfpenny, read Mass for thirteen pence, and at any house he came to [hear] confession, if he got hay and oats for his horse to take it – if not, to go away, on pain of suffering for it.' Dennis Browne, one of the largest landlords in Ireland and a magistrate in Mayo, gave his view of the aims and actions of the Threshers:

> The first object of the association was the reduction of tithes and priests' dues – when it travelled into this part it assumed that, and another shape, that of attacking the wages of weavers and other artificers – and latterly farmers. In different stages of its progress it professed different objects – all kinds of payments, whether of tithes, industry, labour, or farming – assemblies of people collected in disguise and wearing badges and armed, appeared in different parts of the country.
>
> It shewed itself in posting up written notices, exciting people to rebellion under various different pretences. When I took steps in different parts to stop the consequence of these notices, by tearing them down and offering rewards, they adopted another mode of exciting disturbances, by delivering messages in the chapels, threatening the priests, and calling upon the congregations, that if they did not lower their dues – avoid the payment of tithes, and alter the payment of labourers, the *Threshers* would visit them, and that the priests might have their coffins prepared – and that the flesh would be torn off their bones, which messages have had more effect in spreading the mischief, than any mode which was before resorted to.

Ridgeway's report of the special commission proceedings should prove a valuable supplement to such sources as the State of the Country Papers for counties Sligo, Mayo, Leitrim, Longford and Cavan in 1806. Another account of criminal proceedings in the early nineteenth century, *Trials at Omagh, Lifford and Londonderry summer assizes, 1813, before the Hon. Sir W.C. Smith, bart. and Mr Justice Fletcher, the then going judges of assize for the north west circuit* (Dublin, 1815) is important for the light that it throws on the sectarian motives for violence – including murder – at fairs in various parts of north-west Ulster during this period. The published account of the trial of Reverend Valentine Griffith, a magistrate of Queen's County, and Constable James Carroll for the murder of three men at Cardtown fair in June 1814 – the three men were engaged in a fierce faction fight which was suppressed by a party of constabulary acting under the clergyman's orders – provides ample evidence of the similarly ferocious nature of violence at fairs in that part of Leinster at the same time.[95]

More evidence of faction fighting at fairs in Tipperary comes from A. Brewster, *A report of seven trials at the Clonmel summer assizes of MDCCCXXIX, including those which arose out of the occurrences at Borrisokane, on the 26th and 28th of July, 1829* (Dublin, 1830). This voluminous and extremely detailed source, when read with care, opens a window into the mindset of faction fighters in Tipperary in the late 1820s, as well as the murderous animosity that many Catholic peasants felt towards the constabulary and local 'Brunswickers' or 'blue guts' – Protestant opponents of Catholic Emancipation. One of the trials reported on is that of Captain William Henry Pearce for the murder of Paul Slattery, a member of a mob that attacked a party of police and soldiers and tried to seize their arms in Carrick-on-Suir, County Tipperary, on 8 June 1829. The trial evidence shows that Carrick-on-Suir was in uproar on that day. The violence initially involved a riot between opposing members of the 65th and 76th regiments, in a dispute over Catholic Emancipation; or, as the prosecuting counsel, Richard Lalor Sheil put it, 'the merits of Catholic Emancipation went through a process of military review'. After the local constabulary arrested two members of the 65th regiment, their colleagues joined with a mob of townspeople to attack the police. It was in the ensuing mêlée that Slattery was killed. The evidence in Brewster's publication needs to be read with caution and cross-checked or corroborated with evidence from other sources, as it is clear from the cases that he has reported on that perjury or, at the very least, prevarication was rife in these trials. The historian researching crime and disorder in Tipperary in the late 1820s should not discount the evidence that Brewster has provided, then, but will need to exercise keen forensic skills when trying to decide between claim and counter-claim at the Clonmel summer assizes. A similar note of caution applies to approaching many of the sources available for the study of crime in Ireland in this period.[96]

95 William Ridgeway, *A report of the trial of the Rev. Valentine Griffith, and James Carroll, upon three indictments for murder, at the assizes of Maryborough, on the 2d day of August, 1814, before the right hon. Lord Norbury, chief justice of the common pleas* (Dublin, 1814). **96** For a discussion of cases with strong sectarian overtones in which perjured evidence featured in court proceedings see D.S. Johnson, 'The trials of Sam Gray: Monaghan politics and nineteenth century Irish criminal procedure' in *Irish Jurist*, xx, new series (1985), pp 109–34 and Kerby A. Miller, 'The lost world of Andrew Johnston: sectarianism, social conflict, and cultural change in southern Ireland during the pre-Famine era' in James S. Donnelly, jr,

Other recommended published accounts of criminal proceedings in the pre-Famine period include Peter Gorman, *A report of the proceedings under a special commission of oyer and terminer, in the counties of Limerick and Clare, in the months of May and June, 1831, including the proceedings at the adjourned commission in Ennis* (Limerick, 1831),[97] the anonymously authored *Report of the trial of William Kilfoyle, upon the charge of killing Mary Mulrooney at Newtownbarry, on the 18th of June, 1831* (Dublin, 1831) and *Report of the trial of John Kennedy, for the murder of Edward Butler, at Carrickshock, on the 14th December, 1831* (Dublin, 1832). Gorman's publication contains details of numerous cases of agrarian crime in Limerick, Clare, Galway and Roscommon; the defendants in some of these cases were represented by Daniel O'Connell. The details of the evidence against the defendants adds considerably to the material available to the researcher in police and magistrates' reports in the National Archives. The report of the proceedings against William Kilfoyle, a policeman charged with manslaughter, is of particular interest to historians of crime and disorder in Wexford. It contains evidence of witnesses to the affray that arose when the peasantry at Newtownbarry attempted to prevent a party of bailiffs, yeomanry and police from distraining tithe-defaulters' cattle: an estimated twelve to fourteen civilians were shot in disputed circumstances. The report of the trial of John Kennedy concerns the even more notorious tithe affray at Carrickshock, when a party of constabulary that was protecting a process-server was attacked by a huge crowd of peasants. The force suffered its single biggest loss of life in the nineteenth century in this incident.[98] For the Famine years, a particularly valuable source is John Simpson Armstrong, *A report of trials under a special commission for the county of Limerick* (Dublin, 1848). This special commission, which was held in January 1848, dealt with numerous cases of murder, attacking dwelling houses to procure arms or money, and one case of harbouring a notorious murderer, William 'Puck' Ryan, who murdered a neighbouring farmer at Knocksentry in September 1847.

Published accounts of trials are less common for the post-Famine decades, and they tend to focus on individual or isolated crimes that attracted national attention rather than crimes that were part of more general crime waves or disturbances. The fact that this type of source occurs less frequently reflects the fact that the authorities had less recourse to the expedient of special commissions in this period, given the generally more peaceful state of post-Famine Irish society.[99] Publications that are worth noting include the following *causes célèbres*: *Trial of James Spollen, for the murder of Mr George Samuel Little, at the Broadstone terminus of the Midland Great Western Railway, Ireland, August 7th, 8th, 10th & 11th* (Dublin, 1857), *Report of the*

and Kerby A. Miller (eds), *Irish popular culture, 1650–1850* (Dublin, 1998), pp 222–41. **97** Virginia Crossman, 'Emergency legislation and agrarian disorder in Ireland, 1821–41' in *Irish Historical Studies*, xxvii, no. 108 (Nov. 1991), pp 317–18 discusses the background to the holding of this special commission. **98** For an account of the Carrickshock affair see Palmer, *Police and protest*, pp 333–8 and Gary Owens, 'The Carrickshock incident, 1831: social memory and an Irish *cause célèbre*' in *Cultural and Social History*, 1 (2004), pp 36–64. **99** See Mark Finnane, 'A decline of violence in Ireland? Crime, policing and social relations, 1860–1914' in *Crime, histoire et sociétés*, 1, no. 1 (1997), pp 51–70.

trial of Robert Kelly, for the murder of Head-Constable Talbot, at the City of Dublin commission court, October, 1871 (Dublin, 1873), *Full report on the trial and sentence on Tim Kelly for the Phoenix Park murders* (Dublin, n.d.), and *Report of the trials at the Dublin commission court, April and May, 1883, of the prisoners charged with the Phoenix Park murder, the attempt to murder Mr Field, and the conspiracy to murder; before the hon. Mr Justice O'Brien* (Dublin, 1883).

A useful source for the study of agrarian crime and the Land War in County Kilkenny is *Report of the trial of Walter Phelan and John Phelan for murder, in the queen's bench division of the high court of justice in Ireland, before the lord chief justice and a jury of the city of Dublin, June 27, 28, 29, & 30, 1881* (Dublin, 1881). This source provides intimate details of the circumstances surrounding the murder of Charles Boyd on 8 August 1880 at Shanbogh. On that day four members of the Boyd family were ambushed by three armed men and 21-year-old Charles, the son of Thomas Boyd, who was a landlord and crown solicitor for Tipperary, was killed. The 207 pages of evidence in this case provide a good example of how intricate the issues in agrarian cases could be. In this instance the accused were brothers of two men who had been in dispute with their landlord over his revaluation of his lands in 1872, which led to his raising their rent. Philip H. Bagenal, *Crime in Ireland: the winter assizes in Ulster, Munster, Leinster and Connaught, with an appendix* (Dublin, 1880) gives brief summaries of the cases tried at the winter assizes in Ireland in 1880, as well as selected extracts of the trial evidence; for details of criminal cases under the 1887 Coercion Act at the end of the decade, *Judgments of the superior courts in Ireland in cases under the Criminal Law and Procedure (Ireland) Act, and others* (Dublin, 1890) is a useful guide.[1]

The most spectacular use of special commissions in the post-Famine period was the series of trials of Fenian leaders arrested after the suspension of habeus corpus in late 1865 and early 1866, and after the failure of the rebellion in the summer of 1867.[2] The published proceedings of these trials, beginning with that of Thomas Clarke Luby in November 1865,[3] are invaluable for the behind-the-scenes evidence that they provide of Fenianism at local level. Much of the evidence consists of incriminating correspondence seized by the police, and the information of informers. Copies of transcripts of the proceedings are available in the National Library and the Oireachtas Library.[4]

---

[1] For a guide to coercion laws in the nineteenth century see I.S. Leadam, *Coercive measures in Ireland, 1830–1880* (London, 1880) and Crossman, *Politics, law and order*, pp 199–230. [2] R.W. Kostal, 'Rebels in the dock: the prosecution of the Dublin Fenians, 1865–6' in *Éire-Ireland*, xxxiv, no. 2 (summer 1999), pp 70–6. [3] *Report of the proceedings and the first sitting of the special commission for the county of Dublin, held at Green-Street, Dublin, for the trial of Thomas Clarke Luby, and others, for 'treason felony', 'The Fenian conspiracy', commencing on November 27, 1865* (Dublin, 1866). [4] Oireachtas Library, Leinster House, Kildare Street, Dublin 2. The Oireachtas Library holds copies of the published accounts of the January 1866 proceedings against such Fenian leaders as Hugh Francis Brophy, Edward Duffy, William Francis Roantree, Charles J. Kickham and Denis Dowling Mulcahy, as well as eighteen others.

NEWSPAPERS

Newspapers are an important source for the study of crime at local level. There was avid interest in the nineteenth century in accounts of crimes and trials, especially trials at quarter sessions and assizes.[5] Newspapers usually provided detailed coverage of proceedings at county quarter sessions and spring and summer assizes, as well as the more regular local petty sessions, and these details offer a useful additional or alternative source to the official reports of policemen and magistrates, particularly as one can often read in them the defendants' version of events in a more direct form than in police or magistrates' reports. Among the numerous studies of pre-Famine crime, those that are mainly based on a close reading of newspaper evidence include W.A. Maguire's examination of a rape case on the outskirts of Belfast in 1813, Charles Dillon's account of the murder of two Catholics in Crossmaglen, County Armagh, in 1818, Paul Connell's study of the massacre at Castlepollard fair in County Westmeath in 1831 and Réamonn Ó Muirí's account of the killing of another Catholic in Armagh in 1845.[6] Studies of later crime and public disorder that are mainly newspaper based include articles by Donnchadh Ó Ceallacháin, Kevin McMahon and Peter Kerr on the Land War in Waterford, Armagh and Tyrone, respectively, Clare Murphy's work on the anti-grazier disturbances in Connacht in 1911–1912 and Emmet O'Connor's examination of agrarian disturbance in Waterford in the 1917–1923 period.[7]

One needs to be aware that nineteenth- and early twentieth-century newspapers were often politically partisan, and that a newspaper's nationalist or unionist editorial bias coloured its reporting of agrarian or other crime. In the early nineteenth century the Dublin Castle authorities used the secret service fund to bribe newspaper editors or journalists,[8] as well as to finance their own newspapers. Newspapers that were deemed seditious were suppressed or their editors were prosecuted or warned as to their future conduct, which undoubtedly influenced their coverage of agrarian crime, the Tithe War of the 1830s or popular disturbances such

---

5 For the entertainment value that contemporaries derived from newspaper coverage of trials see W.A. Maguire, 'The Verner rape trial, 1813: Jane Barnes v. the Belfast establishment' in *Ulster Local Studies*, 15, no. 1 (summer 1993), p. 47 and Curtin, *Women of Galway jail*, pp 2–3. 6 Maguire, 'Verner rape trial'; Charles Dillon, 'Murder at Aughnacloy 1818' in *Dúiche Néill*, 1, no. 5 (1990), pp 107–32; Paul Connell, '"Slaughtered like wild beasts": massacre at Castlepollard fair, 1831' in Denis A. Cronin, Jim Gilligan and Karina Holton (eds), *Irish fairs and markets: studies in local history* (Dublin, 2001), pp 143–63; Réamonn Ó Muirí, 'Orangemen, Repealers and the shooting of John Boyle in Armagh, 12 July 1845' in *Seanchas Ard Mhacha*, 11, no. 2 (1985), pp 435–529. 7 Donnchadh Ó Ceallacháin, 'Land agitation in County Waterford, 1879–1882' in *Decies*, 53 (1997), pp 91–131; Kevin McMahon, 'The "Crossmaglen conspiracy" case, Part I' in *Seanchas Ard Mhacha*, 6, no. 2 (1972), pp 251–86; idem, 'The "Crossmaglen conspiracy" case, Part II' in *Seanchas Ard Mhacha*, 7, no. 1 (1973), pp 65–107; Peter Kerr, 'Land agitation in Termonmagurk 1885–86' in *Seanchas Ard Mhacha*, 12, no. 2 (1987), pp 149–84; Clare C. Murphy, 'Conflict in the West: the ranch war continues, 1911–1912, Part I' in *Cathair na Mart*, 15 (1995), pp 84–105; idem, 'Conflict in the West: the ranch war continues, part II' in *Cathair na Mart*, 16 (1996), pp 112–39; Emmet O'Connor, 'Agrarian unrest and the Labour movement in County Waterford 1917–1923' in *Saothar*, 6 (1980), pp 40–58. 8 John F. McEldowney, 'Legal aspects of the Irish secret service fund, 1793–1833' in *Irish Historical Studies*, xxv, no. 98 (Nov. 1986), p.133.

as election riots, for instance.⁹ Throughout the Union period, then, the press had to be wary of antagonising Dublin Castle, although one can discount the view of Richard Pigott, the proprietor of the *Irishman* and *Flag of Ireland* newspapers, that in the 1870s freedom of the press had been 'utterly annihilated' in Ireland.¹⁰ Newspapers with quite inflammatory views, such as the Fenians' *Irish People* in the 1860s or William O'Brien's *United Ireland* in the 1880s, could remain unmolested for several years before the authorities took action against them, providing a useful counterweight to unionist journals such as the *Irish Times* in their coverage of crime and criminal trials. A number of secondary sources offer useful information on newspapers' political bias, as well as their areas of circulation, for a selected number of years in the nineteenth and early twentieth centuries.¹¹

A more wide-ranging guide to Irish newspapers in the period is James O'Toole (ed.), *Newsplan: report of the newsplan project in Ireland* (London and Dublin, 1992). This provides an alphabetical listing of Irish newspapers, as well as details of the library or other institution where they are held, the runs available, and whether these are available on microfilm or in hardcopy. While it is the best published guide it is not comprehensive, as its narrow definition of a newspaper as 'a daily or weekly publication carrying general news' which 'is not the organ of a particular party or group'¹² means that some important sources for the study of subversive or illegal activity in the twentieth century are not included. Most of the newspapers listed in the *Newsplan* are available in the National Library of Ireland or the British Library's Newspaper Library at Colindale, London.¹³ The National Library also has an alphabetical list of its Irish newspaper holdings at the issue desk.

Scarcely any Irish newspapers of this period are indexed, unfortunately; an exception to the rule is the *Downpatrick Recorder*, which has been indexed for the years 1836 to 1886.¹⁴ The *Times* (London) frequently published accounts of Irish crime, especially agrarian cases. There are a number of indexes to the *Times* in this period: from 1790 to 1905 there are quarterly indexes for each year; the quarterly system was replaced by an annual alphabetical index covering the entire year's reports in 1906.¹⁵ One can also find material of Irish interest in the indexes of the *Illustrated London News*, particularly for the years of the Land War.

The newspapers that will prove most useful to the researcher of crime at local level will vary according to the period, location and type of crime being researched.

---

9 Brian Inglis, *The freedom of the press in Ireland, 1784–1841* (London, 1954). **10** Richard Pigott, *Personal recollections of an Irish national journalist* (Dublin, 1883), p. 331. **11** Inglis, *Freedom of the press*, pp 239–42; Marie-Louise Legg, *Newspapers and nationalism: the Irish provincial press, 1850–1892* (Dublin, 1999), pp 177–222; Virginia E. Glandon, *Arthur Griffith and the advanced-nationalist press in Ireland, 1900–1922* (New York, 1985), pp 252–304. **12** O'Toole, *Newsplan*, p. v. **13** British Library Newspaper Library, Colindale Avenue, London NW9 5HE. **14** Jack McCoy, *An index to the Downpatrick Recorder, 1836–1886* (Ballynahinch, 1987). A computerised index of the *Leinster Leader* is currently being created for every year since its founding in 1880. For details see Mary Carroll, '*Leinster Leader* indexation project' in *Journal of the Kildare Archaeological Society*, xxviii, no. 2 (1994–95), pp 259–62. **15** *Palmer's index to The Times newspaper* (London, 1790–1905); *The annual index to The Times* (London, 1906–14); *The official index to The Times* (London, 1914–57).

Regional or even national newspapers may also prove useful to the historian studying a specific crime or series of crimes at local level. The *Cork Examiner*, for instance, published accounts of judicial proceedings at special commissions, assizes, quarter sessions and petty sessions throughout Munster, and many national newspapers such as the *Freeman's Journal* contain accounts of spring and summer assizes throughout Ireland. Even the *Irishman* newspaper, whose main focus was on political proceedings, can prove a gem to the local historian studying crime. For instance, its issue for 17 September 1864 contains a lengthy account of a case of fraud at Carrick-on-Suir petty sessions, in which a supposed 'witch', Mary Doheny, was charged with obtaining money under false pretences from Sub-constable Joseph Reeves and his wife. The defendant, who was apparently a 'healer' who had been attending the couple's sick child, convinced the pair that another child of theirs, a seven-year-old son, who died in 1860, had come back to life and was (in the words of the policeman) 'amongst the gentry' or 'good people' at the 'moat' (presumably a rath) of Ballydine. Keeping their son company at Ballydine was the sub-constable's deceased father-in-law and sister-in-law, and other deceased people known to the married couple: the resurrected dead desired, at various times, money, tobacco, clothing, tea and food, which were to be conveyed to them by the defendant! Another newspaper with a national circulation, the *Irish People* – the Fenian organ – is very revealing of IRB activities at local level when read with care, especially the readers' letters to the editor.[16]

The tone and content of newspaper reports of local crime varies. One of the most sober sources is the police gazette, the *Hue and Cry*. It gives minimal details of crimes, but is useful in that it features physical descriptions of the people whom the police suspected of committing these crimes. Some newspapers tend towards sensationalist accounts, particularly when describing agrarian crimes and the trials of those suspected of committing them. Others, at various times, favoured a humorous approach, especially when reporting on proceedings at petty sessions – for instance, accounts in certain Mayo newspapers from the late 1820s to the early 1840s,[17] the *Freeman's Journal* when describing cases of non-indictable crime in Dublin in the 1860s, particularly drunk and disorderly cases, or the *Waterford News* when reporting similar petty sessions cases in the early 1890s. When read with care, however, such accounts can be very revealing of crime at the local level in the cities, towns and rural areas of Ireland.

In addition to newspapers themselves, a number of collections of newspaper articles were published in book form during the Land War and these often deal with

---

16 For a discussion of the *Irish People* see O'Leary, *Recollections of Fenians*, passim; Marcus Bourke, *John O'Leary: a study in Irish separatism* (Tralee, 1967), pp 50–84; R.V. Comerford, *Charles J. Kickham: a study in Irish nationalism and literature* (Dublin, 1979), pp 66–78. For an example of an article that is based largely on the files of the *Irish People* see Brian Griffin, '"Scallions, pikes and bog oak ornaments": the Irish Republican Brotherhood and the Chicago Fenian Fair, 1864' in *Studia Hibernica*, no. 29 (1995–97), pp 85–97. **17** Desmond McCabe, 'Law, conflict and social order: County Mayo 1820–1845' (unpublished PhD thesis, University College Dublin, 1991), pp 79–80.

crime and agrarian disorder. The more useful include Finlay Dun, *Landlords and tenants in Ireland* (London, 1881) – a collection of reports written for the *Times* during the winter of 1880; E. Cant-Wall, *Ireland under the Land Act* (London, 1882), which comprises the author's reports to the *Standard* newspaper in 1881; the anonymously authored *The letters of 'Norah' on her tour through Ireland* (Montreal, 1882), which consists of the despatches from the *Montreal Witness*'s Ireland special correspondent to her newspaper in 1881; Bernard Becker, *Disturbed Ireland: being the letters written during the winter of 1880–1881* (London, 1881), a compilation of reports by the *Daily Mail*'s special correspondent; the anonymously authored *Letters from Ireland, 1886* (London, 1887), which consists of reports published in the *Times* in 1886 and H. Whitfield, *Mr Balfour's instruments and victims, being a tour of experiences of coercion and eviction as encountered during a tour of Ireland* (Plymouth, 1888) and *Who are the conspirators? or Ireland's criminals and their crimes* (Plymouth, 1889), by the editor of the *Western Daily Mercury*. Henry Norman's *Bodyke: a chapter in the history of Irish landlordism* (London, 1887) is based on the author's despatches to the *Pall Mall Gazette* while he was covering the Plan of Campaign in 1887.

Timothy Harrington's propaganda work, *A diary of coercion* (Dublin, 1888), which gives details of the cases tried under the Criminal Law and Jurisdiction Act from 17 August 1887 to 16 March 1888, republishes numerous newspaper accounts of many of the trials. Another valuable source of propaganda which relies heavily on newspaper extracts was produced by the anti-Home Rule and anti-National League body, the Irish Loyal and Patriotic Union. The ILPU's pamphlets drew on nationalist newspaper coverage of the Plan of Campaign and associated crime and criminal proceedings. Together with Harrington's book, they constitute graphic sources for researching the Land War of the late 1880s. Among the most useful pamphlets are *Ireland under the ordinary law: a record of the agrarian crimes and offences reported in the Dublin daily press, for the six months running from 1st October, 1886, to 31st March, 1887* (Dublin, London and Edinburgh, 1887), *Ireland in 1887: Part I, Proceedings at assizes; Part II, Extracts from proceedings of National League branches* (Dublin and London, 1887), and *1879–88: the sanction of a creed; a short record of murders and attempts at murder in Ireland since the institution of the Irish National Land League* (Dublin and London, 1888). A useful later publication from the Irish Unionist Alliance, *Cattle-driving in Ireland* (Dublin, 1908) also reproduces numerous extracts from contemporary Irish newspapers, as well as photographs illustrating the extraordinary measures to which the authorities resorted in order to protect graziers in various parts of Ireland during the early twentieth-century anti-grazier agitation.

Another important source of newspaper coverage of crime, disorder and subversive activity (as defined by the Dublin Castle authorities) is the collection of newspaper cuttings compiled by the under-secretary for Ireland, Thomas Larcom, in the 1850s and 1860s. Of special interest are the volumes on Fenianism, the Belfast riots of 1864 and agrarian crime in various counties.[18] The Chief Secretary's Office collection of newspaper cuttings in the National Library should also prove valuable

---

18 Details of the Larcom Papers may be found in Hayes, *Manuscript sources*.

to the researcher. Consisting of some 194 bound volumes and covering the period from 1880 to 1920, this source comprises cuttings relating to the activities of such organisations as the Land League, the Gaelic League, the United Irish League, the Ulster and Irish Volunteers, the Suffragette movement[19] and Sinn Féin. Other volumes contain cuttings concerning evictions on the Aran islands and priests' speeches on a wide range of political and other subjects. The collection is of use insofar as it gives the researcher convenient access to a wide range of newspaper material, providing leads that one could follow up by cross-checking in other issues and newspapers not contained in the collection.[20] The student of the War of Independence in Armagh, Down and Louth will find Kevin McMahon's collection of verbatim reports from the *Newry Reporter*, *Dundalk Democrat*, *Armagh Guardian* and *Frontier Sentinel* of particular interest.[21]

---

19 For a discussion of crimes committed as part of the campaign to achieve women's suffrage see Rosemary Cullen Owens, *Smashing times: a history of the Irish women's suffrage movement, 1889–1922* (Dublin, 1984), pp 55–73. **20** Researchers should note that the National Library's computer catalogue gives inaccurate details of this collection, and that they should consult the bound catalogues instead. **21** Kevin McMahon, 'The time of the trouble 1919–21: Armagh, South Down and North Louth part 1' in *Seanchas Ard Mhacha*, 15, no. 1 (1992), pp 217–71; idem, 'The time of the trouble 1919–21: Armagh, South Down and North Louth part 2' in *Seanchas Ard Mhacha*, 16, no. 1 (1994), pp 195–235; idem, 'The time of the trouble 1919–21: Armagh, South Down and North Louth part 3' in *Seanchas Ard Mhacha*, 17, no. 1 (1996–97), pp 163–93.

Conclusion

The preceding discussion of the sources for the study of crime and disorder in nineteenth- and early twentieth-century Ireland reveals a number of recurrent features, which the researcher will have to come to terms with when engaging in his or her study of these subjects. Firstly, the vast bulk of the material that is available to the researcher comes from officials whose job was either to prevent or detect crime or to prosecute lawbreakers. There was often a huge gulf between the perspectives of these officials and the points of view of those who broke the law. One should entertain the possibility that when policemen, magistrates and other prosecutors assigned motives to criminals and political agitators or described their actions, they were influenced by feelings of hostility which led to their distorting or misrepresenting the motives or actions of the latter. Another consideration to bear in mind is that officials, whose primary loyalty was to the state, may simply have been unable to fully appreciate the complex motives of the agrarian lawbreaker whose primary loyalty was variously to class, family, locality or community. Other contemporaries, such as travellers or newspaper editors and journalists, were also outsiders to the peasant community and their accounts of rural crime, especially collective crime perceived as having some form of tacit communal approval, may also provide partial or distorted evidence for the researcher to assess. One of the main frustrations and challenges for the researcher, then, is that the primary sources rarely provide firsthand or unmediated evidence from real or suspected lawbreakers. This is not to say that it is impossible for one to gain a reasonably full understanding of crime in the period under discussion. The vast machinery of law and order which was operated and administered by the British state in Ireland has provided plenty of primary material which one can, when one bears in mind its inherent biases, still use in conjunction with other contemporary sources to arrive at a reasonable understanding of the nature and causes of crime and disorder.

The second main point that strikes one about the nature of the surviving evidence is that much of it focuses on organised agrarian crime and disorder, or the activities of illegal separatist organisations. Most of the surviving evidence from the pre-Famine period focuses on agrarian crime and disorder; while this still remains a central focus in the post-Famine period, especially from 1879 to the early 1890s, the activities of subversive political organisations also become an increasingly important preoccupation of policemen and other contemporary observers. However, considerably more evidence relating to 'ordinary' or non-political offences, or offences that were not part of communal or collective action, exists for the post-Famine period than the pre-Famine period. While the bulk of historical research on the post-Famine decades has concentrated on such topics as the Fenian movement, the Land War and the War of Independence, the material exists to facilitate the study of 'ordinary' crime. Obvious gaps in the historical record include studies of such topics as drunkenness, juvenile crime, infanticide and sexual assaults:[1] all of these important subjects could be elucidated by drawing on the sources discussed above in this guide. These could be studied at the local level, or the source material could also facilitate more general investigations. However, if one's preference is to study the well-ploughed field of collective agrarian crime or political conspiracy or rebellion, there are still plenty of worthwhile topics for the local historian to explore. For the pre-Famine period, for instance, the Terry Alt movement in Clare from 1828 to 1831 still awaits a full scholarly study, while the topic of crime during the Famine years is neglected for most areas of the country. A local perspective also promises to reward the historian of crime and political subversion in post-Famine and early twentieth-century Ireland. While progress has been made in exploring the activities of rank and file members of the IRB in various parts of Ireland, more studies of the local dimension of Fenianism are still needed, particularly in Ulster. More local studies of agrarian crime in Ulster are also needed,[2] as are studies of the Land War in most parts of the country. For the War of Independence years, more local studies of the activities of the IRA, along the lines of those discussed in the introduction to this guide, are required before a fuller understanding of the nature of that particular conflict is possible. The local study, therefore, holds out the hope of testing historians' generalisations about crime, disorder and political violence during the Union period and making possible a more nuanced understanding of these topics.

---

[1] The latter topic has been explored for the eighteenth century by James Kelly, '"A most inhuman and barbarous piece of villainy": an exploration of the crime of rape in eighteenth-century Ireland' in *Eighteenth-century Ireland*, x (1995), pp 78–107. [2] R.W. Kirkpatrick, 'Origins and development of the Land War in mid-Ulster, 1879–85' in Lyons and Hawkins (eds), *Ireland under the Union*, pp 201–35 is a useful start.

Select bibliography

Abbott, Richard, *Police casualties in Ireland, 1919–1922* (Cork and Dublin, 2000).
Beames, M.R., 'Rural conflict in pre-Famine Tipperary: peasant assassinations in Tipperary, 1837–1847' in *Past & Present*, no. 81 (1978), pp 75–91.
——, *Peasants and power: the Whiteboy movements and their control in pre-Famine Ireland* (Brighton and New York, 1983).
Bew, Paul, *Land and the national question in Ireland, 1858–82* (Dublin, 1978).
Bourke, Angela, *The burning of Bridget Cleary: a true story* (London, 1999).
Broeker, Galen, *Rural disorder and police reform in Ireland, 1812–1836* (London, 1970).
Brownrigg, Henry John, *Examination of some recent allegations concerning the constabulary force in Ireland, in a report to his excellency the lord lieutenant* (Dublin, 1864).
Campbell, Fergus, 'The hidden history of the Irish Land War: a guide to local sources' in Carla King (ed.), *Famine, land and culture in Ireland* (Dublin, 2000), pp 140–53.
Clark, Samuel, 'The importance of agrarian classes: agrarian class structure and collective action in nineteenth-century Ireland' in *British Journal of Sociology*, 29, no. 1 (Mar. 1978), pp 22–40.
——, *Social origins of the Irish Land War* (Princeton, 1979).
Coleman, Anne, *Riotous Roscommon: social unrest in the 1840s* (Dublin, 1999).
Conley, Carolyn A, 'Irish criminal records, 1865–1892' in *Éire-Ireland*, xxviii (1993), pp 97–106.
——, *Melancholy accidents: the meaning of violence in post-Famine Ireland* (Lanham, 1999).
Connell, K.H., 'Illicit distillation' in K.H. Connell, *Irish peasant society: four historical essays* (Oxford, 1968), pp 1–50.
Donnelly, jr, James S., 'The social composition of agrarian rebellions in early nineteenth-century Ireland: the case of the Carders and Caravats, 1813–16' in Patrick J. Corish (ed.), *Radicals, rebels and establishments* (Belfast, 1985), pp 151–69.
——, 'The Terry Alt movement 1829–31' in *History Ireland*, 2, no. 4 (winter 1994), pp 30–5.
Fitzpatrick, David, 'Class, family and agrarian unrest in nineteenth-century Ireland' in P.J. Drudy (ed.), *Irish Studies 2: Ireland: land, politics and people* (Cambridge, 1982), pp 37–75.
——, *Politics and Irish life: provincial experience of war and revolution* (Dublin, 1977).
Gibbons, Stephen, *Captain Rock, night errant: the threatening letters of pre-Famine Ireland, 1801–1845* (Dublin, 2004).
Griffin, Brian, *The Bulkies: police and crime in Belfast, 1800–1865* (Dublin, 1997).
Hart, Peter, *The IRA and its enemies: violence and community in Cork, 1916–1923* (Oxford, 1998).
Lane, Pádraig G., 'Agricultural labourers and rural violence, 1850–1914' in *Studia Hibernica*, no. 27 (1993), pp 77–87.
Lee, Joseph, 'The Ribbonmen' in T. Desmond Williams (ed.), *Secret societies in Ireland* (Dublin, 1973), pp 26–35.
Lewis, George Cornewall, *On local disturbances in Ireland; and on the Irish Church question* (London, 1836).
Mac Giolla Choille, Breandán, 'Fenian documents in the State Paper Office' in *Irish Historical Studies*, xvi, no. 63 (1969), pp 258–84.
Murray, A.C., 'Agrarian violence and nationalism in nineteenth-century Ireland: the myth of Ribbonism' in *Irish Economic and Social History*, 13 (1986), pp 56–73.
Murtagh, Anne, *Portrait of a Westmeath tenant community, 1879–85: the Barbavilla murder* (Dublin, 1999).
Murphy O'Hanlon, William, *Walks among the poor of Belfast* (Belfast and Dublin, 1853).
Palmer, Stanley H., *Police and protest in England and Ireland, 1780–1850* (Cambridge, 1998).
Roberts, Paul E.W., 'Caravats and Shanavests: Whiteboyism and faction fighting in east Munster, 1802–11' in Samuel Clark and James S. Donnelly, jr (eds), *Irish peasants: violence and political unrest 1780–1914* (Madison and Manchester, 1983), pp 64–101.

Satsuta, Shunsuke, 'The Rockite movement in County Cork in the early 1820s' in *Irish Historical Studies*, xxxiii, no. 131 (May 2003), pp 278–96.
Steiner-Scott, Elizabeth, '"To bounce a boot off her now & then ... "': domestic violence in post-Famine Ireland' in Maryann Gialanella Valiulis and Mary O'Dowd (eds), *Women in Irish history: essays in honour of Margaret MacCurtain* (Dublin, 1997), pp 125–43.
Sweeney, Frank, *The murder of Conell Boyle, County Donegal, 1898* (Dublin, 2002).
Townshend, Charles, *Political violence in Ireland: government and resistance since 1848* (Oxford, 1983).
Vaughan, W.E., *Landlords and tenants in mid-Victorian Ireland* (Oxford, 1994).
Waldron, Jarlath, *Maamtrasna: the murders and the mystery* (Dublin, 1992).